# "Where Can We Go This Weekend?"

# "Where Can We Go This Weekend?"

## 154 one, two, and three day travel adventures in Northern California

INCLUDES MONTHLY EVENTS CALENDAR

## by Amy Rennert

**JEREMY P. TARCHER, INC.**
**Los Angeles**
Distributed by Houghton Mifflin Company
Boston

Library of Congress Catalog Card No.: 80–51223

Jeremy P. Tarcher, Inc.
9110 Sunset Blvd.
Los Angeles, CA 90069

Manufactured in the United States of America

G   10   9   8   7   6   5   4   3   2

# Contents

Without George Lowe (Alan R. McElwain), this book would not exist. It was his Southern California *"Where Can We Go This Weekend?"* that got this author started on the right foot.

Special thanks also to Anita Ginsburg, who helped take this book from A to Z, and Liz Metzger, who knows the Gold Country better than anyone else I know.

Jeremy Tarcher, my publisher, and Michael Larsen and Elizabeth Pomada, my agents, are three people every writer should have the privilege of working with.

Thanks also to all the friends who accompanied me on the thousands of miles of travel. At least half the fun and excitement of adventures comes from sharing them.

# FOREWORD

Adventure is the key word for this guide. As far as I'm concerned, that's what traveling is all about.

I always hear friends say how wonderful San Francisco is because, in addition to what the city itself has to offer, a half-hour ride in any direction leads to beautiful sights, interesting people and places, and exciting activities. But how many people really make time to take to the road? It took me, a transplanted Easterner, 4 years to set out exploring Northern California.

And I've only just begun.

# HOW TO USE THIS BOOK

If this book arouses enough of your interest to get you to enjoy some of the adventures to be met in exploring the beautiful, scenic, and interesting Northern California countryside, it will have accomplished its purpose.

Features of similar interest have been placed together so that you may better pick and choose to find the sights and experiences that intrigue you. For example, if exploring little (and sometimes little-known) towns is a high priority on your weekend trips, then Chapter 6 will be of special interest. Or if nature walks and hikes are a special attraction, Chapter 15 should be one of the first sections you read.

In the chapter "Recommended Weekend Adventures" and the Index by Area, we have cut across the lines that separate various interests and grouped together the most interesting things to see and do in specific geographical areas. These sections are designed so that you can easily determine which events and attractions are in the area you've chosen to visit. If you're visiting wineries in Napa County, for instance, you can also take a scenic drive on a back road to Sonoma Valley and/or visit the House of Happy Walls in the Jack London State Park.

Mileages given begin at San Francisco's Golden Gate Bridge or at the Bay Bridge, depending on where you're headed. Trips to Marin County start at the Golden Gate Bridge; those to the East Bay begin at the Bay Bridge. Depending on where you live or where you're staying, you may vary the suggested routes and adjust the mileage accordingly. Unless round trip is specified, all mileages are one-way. (Often the number of miles is not indicative of how long the trip will take. Be sure to check ahead and see the roads and freeways traveled.)

Please note that the kind of information presented in this book is subject to change. Restaurants close and new ones open. Museums change their hours and adventure businesses go out of business. Everything included in this book was accurate at the time of printing, but you may find one or two listings already dated despite our best efforts. It's a good idea to call ahead and double check location and hours before you set out on your adventure.

# TIPS FOR PLEASANT TRAVEL

Here are a few simple rules and suggestions for greater travel enjoyment during the jaunts you will be taking.

*Use a map.* This may seem like obvious advice, but relatively few people actually plan their trips with a map in hand. All kinds of interesting information can be found in some of the excellent road atlases for sale (from the Rand McNally map store at 595 Market Street, (415) 362-4834, or Thomas Brothers Maps at 550 Jackson Street, (415) 981-7520) and from the superb maps that are available to members of automobile clubs. Some of the maps sold by service stations are also very good.

The information on these maps includes the designation of public beaches (and those that have surfing, boat rentals, and sports fishing), the location of old missions and churches, and other places of interest. Look at the box marked "Legend" (generally in a corner of the map) for the various symbols and highway markings. In addition, most maps print next to the highway the mileage between towns and junctions. This information can be very valuable in planning refreshment and rest stops and in estimating the travel time. The California State Automobile Association can also be of tremendous assistance. Call (415) 565-2012.

*Ask directions.* You may have seen the TV commercial in which a man drives around and around the block looking for an address because he is embarrassed to ask for directions. Don't follow his lead. Besides being able to get directions at any gas station, during the same stop you can pick up information about local road conditions and points of interest that are not indicated on the map.

*Keep the tank full.* Whenever the gas gauge drops below half-full, fill up your tank. Not only will doing so keep you from running out of gas and starting your trip on an unpleasant note, but it will also give you an opportunity to get your windows cleaned and oil checked. (Important note: The odd-even regulations about special "gas days" don't apply to travelers more than 100 miles from home.)

Also, make sure you have the emergency supplies you need: spare tire and jack, flares, etc. An automobile club membership is useful for roadside service in remote areas.

***Plan ahead***. It's a good idea to plan your trip far enough ahead of time so you have a chance to write the Chamber of Commerce at your destination. Local maps, lists of hotels, motels, restaurants, folders describing things to see and do locally—all manner of material will come to you by return mail. You may discover that your trip coincides with a convention or large festival, and you will have a chance to make advance reservations—or find out there are none available when you want to arrive.

***A picnic kit is handy***. An airline flight bag makes an ideal inexpensive picnic kit. If you travel frequently, keep a bag stocked and ready with plastic plates, knives, forks, spoons, small drinking cups, salt and pepper shakers, packets of condiments and instant beverages. Even a small can of meat spread and a box of crackers will permit spur-of-the-moment picnicking if the local eating places do not appear inviting. It can be a great deal of fun to stop at a grocery store for tomatoes, lettuce, cold meats, cheese, milk, etc., and make yourself a roadside feast.

***Other handy supplies***. Obviously, if you're a camera buff, you should have an extra supply of film along (keep it out of the hot glove compartment or trunk). If you're an artist, you'll want to bring drawing paper and art equipment. Writers will want to carry journals. If you're traveling with children, take one or several plastics bags filled with items to keep them occupied. Coloring books, magnetic puzzles, cards, pipe cleaners, and finger puppets are some things the kids can use during driving time; they can play with balls, frisbees, and sand toys during picnic stops. Fruit, cheese, and snacks that don't melt in your car will make the trip more comfortable; so will pillows and blankets. Bathing suits and towels can also come in handy, if you find a camp site or a motel that has a swimming pool. If you're going to be away overnight and like to read in bed, carry a good plug-in lamp or a 150-watt light bulb to avoid going blind under dim motel lamps. Flashlights are essential for camping.

***Avoid the traffic jam***. Even if this means getting an early start in the morning, try to schedule your travel so that you're off the road by 3 o'clock on Sunday afternoon. That's usually when the homeward rush becomes crushing on many highways. Don't spoil a delightful weekend by inching for hours, bumper to bumper, on a jammed highway. Experienced travelers, if they find themselves caught in the traffic, know they can stop at a pleasant place and enjoy a leisurely dinner, then complete the trip after the traffic has thinned—which, on certain highways, may mean quite late at night.

*Relax.* Above all, take it easy and relax. As soon as you get off the freeway, slow down and enjoy the countryside. If a speedster is tailgating you, pull over to the side and let him pass.

Set up your schedule loosely enough to allow unexpected stops along the way for anything that might interest you. At a slow pace you'll see many interesting things that you'd otherwise miss—a big hawk on a telephone pole, calves or lambs with their mothers by the roadside, a beautiful sunset—things like these are what you left the city for. Give yourself time to enjoy them.

# 1—LITTLE ADVENTURES

You don't have to travel far to find adventure in Northern California. You can canoe or inner tube down a creek or snowshoe to the warm waters of Grover Hot Springs within a few hours from home, or ride on one of San Francisco's famous cable cars in the city itself.

Some adventures have a high price tag; others, often just as exciting, don't cost a cent.

## 1—A    This Bridge Was Made for Walking

A walk across the Golden Gate Bridge is always a thrilling experience. The bridge's design and setting are unlike any in the world. Both ends have beautiful coastal panoramas, with the Marin headlands to the north and San Francisco sparkling to the south. As a pedestrian you can enjoy views beneath you that the auto traveler misses.

The bridge seems almost alive as it gives and sways from the enormous weight of the road and thousands of vehicles. No cause for alarm, however. Because of its windy location and anticipated heavy use, the Golden Gate was designed to be the most durable bridge ever built. The bridge was constructed over a 4-year period, along with the two gigantic towers that rise 746 feet above the water. It stretches 1.7 miles and cost $35 million. The center span—suspended over water 318 feet deep—is 4,200 feet wide. Every year, the bridge gets a new coat (10,000 gallons) of "international orange" paint.

First opened in 1937, the bridge now takes cars, trucks, buses, pedestrians, and runners across the Bay (roller skaters are still prohibited). In late October, the Embarcadero YMCA sponsors a Golden Gate Marathon. Thousands of runners cross the bridge while equal numbers of would-be runners and fans enjoy the spectacle.

There are places to park and observation areas on both sides of the bridge. If you cross by bicycle, you might want to continue on to Sausalito (see 4-D) and then board the ferry at the front of Anchor Street for your return trip.

## 1–B  Watch Out for Big Bertha

Big Bertha is the name of the roughest set of rapids on Cache Creek, which runs through the small town of Guinda (about 35 miles north of Vacaville). Not many people have discovered this wonderful 4-mile run. The ones who have, hope it doesn't become too popular, and they are reluctant to give away their secret.

Inner tubing can be either a solitary or a group adventure—you can drift at your own pace or ride bumper-to-bumper with friends. But there's a real art to it, and unless you master it you may return from the rapids with a bruised bottom. While you're coasting along, remember to let the tire protect you. Don't drag your bottom or lower back or the rocks will give you a beating. In between rapids, on the calm stretches of water, you can get more comfortable and even swim alongside your tube.

The best time of year for this sport is the summer, when the water level is best. Below 6 inches will put you on the rocks, and when they're over a foot deep, the rushing waters can be hazardous.

Riding this creek is free, but you may have to purchase a few items ahead of time. Large used truck inner tubes can be found in the yellow pages under "Tires," and price-comparison shopping may get you one for under $5. Life jackets should be purchased at surplus stores. Sneakers and suntan lotion are a must. A stem remover for $1.50 (buy this along with the inner tube) will deflate tires at the end of the day.

To do this trip right, you'll need at least two cars, so the best plan is to go with a group. Park one car at the starting point and one where you plan to wind up. A third car in between can serve as a lunch stop. (You can try attaching some liquid refreshments to your inner tube with some string, but they may not make it through the trip.)

Take Interstate 80 to Vacaville, then go north on Interstate 505 for 20 miles to Highway 16. Travel through Esparto and Capay, then pick your spot. Approximately 95 miles. Allow two hours' driving time.

## 1–C  Snow Hikes in the Sierra

A snowshoe hike up Hot Springs Creek to wintry waterfalls and an overnight trek to a snow cave are two of several free guided snow hikes offered in the Lake Tahoe area (see 12-B).

Both novice and experienced snowshoers and cross-country skiers can take advantage of the 3- or 4-hour tours and overnight trips offered in November and from

January through March. These trips are sponsored by the State Department of Parks and Recreation.

The picturesque hike up Hot Springs Creek is moderately difficult. It's a 4-mile, 4-hour trip with a 600-foot elevation gain. A dip in the hot springs at the trip's end will soothe and relax sore muscles. (You'll need a swimsuit and towel for this.)

An easier hike takes cross-country skiers and snowshoers on fairly level ground through the Sugar Pine Point State Park. You'll learn about this area's history during the 4-hour walk along the shore of Lake Tahoe.

For newcomers to cross-country skiing, an introductory session includes a demonstration of equipment and ski-waxing techniques followed by an easy 2-mile practice walk at 6,000 feet.

Advanced cross-country skiers can hike 5 miles, from 5,900 feet to 7,000 feet, on Scallenberger Ridge. You'll definitely want a camera for some of the views on your way down.

The overnight survival hike at Sugar Pine Point State Park covers 4 miles at 6,200 feet. If there's enough snow, trekkers sleep in snow caves; otherwise you'll need a tent. There's also a daytime survival trip, which includes a talk and a demonstration of survival equipment.

All trips are led by park personnel trained in natural history. You can rent equipment for the hikes locally or in Truckee on the way there. For day trips, plan to bring lunch and something to drink. For overnighters, you'll need a sleeping bag and pad, change of clothes, a stove, and possibly a tent. Always wear sturdy clothing that will protect you from the cold and moisture. Kids under 16 must be accompanied by an adult.

For a complete listing of the trips, and to make reservations, write to the Sierra Area State Parks, P.O. Drawer D, Tahoma, California 95733, or phone (916) 525-7232 between 8 A.M. and 4:30 P.M. on weekdays.

The Sierra Area Parks also have a Spring/Summer Hike Schedule, so you can request specifics on those trips too.

## 1–D    Secret Swims

If you've been disappointed not to find more swimmable ocean beaches (see 3-C) in Northern California, don't despair. Instead discover the beauty of local swimming holes.

Almost any town or resort area near a body of water is sure to have special dunking spots. Johnson's Beach, just below a bridge in Guerneville (approximately 65 miles from San Francisco) is one of these. Families love this spot; it's safe for kids because lifeguards are on duty from 10 A.M. to 6 P.M. until October 1.

Some places are a little more difficult to locate but well worth looking for.

A personal favorite is the Steely Fork swimming hole in Steely Creek. Take Interstates 80 and 50 to Placerville, then take Highway 49 south for 3 miles. Turn left onto Pleasant Valley Road, then travel 4½ miles to Bucks Bar Road. Turn right and continue until it becomes Grizzly Flat Road. About 7 miles further along you'll see an old green farm on your left. Larry Williamson lives there and owns the property, and he likes swimmers to drop by before dunking. Another tenth of a mile takes you to the bridge, where you can park and then hike across the highway and down a few hundred yards to the creek.

The cool waters of Steely Creek are surrounded by smooth granite rocks, perfect for diving because the water is fairly deep. The cold water and bright sun are a delightful combination; you'll probably want to stay for hours.

Approximately 125 miles.

You'll find another swimming hole below an old cement bridge in the Oregon Creek Campground in Tahoe National Forest. It's a deep pool perfect for swimming and diving off rocks, but not deep enough to chance jumping off the bridge. For less serious swimmers there are several small sandy beaches and shallow areas for wading close by, along with picnicking facilities and campsites.

East and north via Interstate 80 and Highway 49 (pick up 49 in Auburn). Follow 49 for 18 miles past Nevada City to the Oregon Creek Campground. Approximately 135 miles.

Finally, if and when you take a rafting trip, be sure to have your river rafting guides lead you to their favorite swimming holes along the Stanislaus (see 2-A).

## 1—E    The City's Rollercoaster

For many people, a visit to San Francisco is not the real thing without a cable car ride. The cable car is the oldest urban transit system, first introduced in 1873. The cars have retained their charm, but mechanical problems have sometimes kept them from clanging away for up to months at a time.

A cable car ride is one of the unique experiences San Francisco has to offer. The gripmen running the cars at 9½ miles an hour take pride in their work, and most will readily answer questions or tell stories about the old days.

At one time women were prohibited from standing on the outside step of the car because it was considered too dangerous, not to mention unladylike. (By the way, the outside step is the most exciting place to be. Just hang on tight as the car makes those right-angle turns.) Later, during the 1950s, there was an attempt to abolish the entire system. Some of the cable cars were phased out then, but public interest has insured that three routes remain.

Passengers can ride from Market and Powell Streets over the steep Nob and Russian Hill neighborhoods out to the Fisherman's Wharf area. The views are spectacular, especially on the No. 60 Powell-Hyde line. The third line runs along California Street through the financial district and Chinatown, up Nob Hill and finally out to Van Ness Street.

All three lines are operated by huge 14-foot wheels in the cable car barn on the corner of Washington and Mason Streets. From the gallery visitors can watch the wheels in motion and learn more about the cars and how they run (and break down). Old photographs and pieces of equipment are also on display and, if the cars aren't running during your visit to the city, this is the only place you can still sit or stand on the outside step of a cable car. The museum hours are 10 A.M. to 5 P.M. seven days a week. There is no charge.

The cars run from 6 A.M. until 1 A.M., but the best time to take a ride is early in the morning. Otherwise you might find yourself waiting in lines longer than those for the best movies in town.

Nowhere in the world is there another system like the San Francisco cable cars. For 50¢ you can have a unique thrill. Don't miss it.

## 1—F    Sightsee on Waterskis

Waterskiing is the San Joaquin Delta's most popular water sport. If you can afford about $70 a day or $16 per hour, plus gas, for a boat that carries five people, you can enjoy endless hours of fun. The waterskiing is best in the wide-open straight channels, but be sure to get a map; without one, you'll have a tough time finding your way back to your starting point.

With the scene changing around every bend on the waterways, beginners may have a difficult time concentrating on keeping their skis together. But both beginners and experts will love every minute.

When arm and leg muscles begin to tire, or you merely want a change of pace, you can cruise quietly along or pull over to your own beach for swims, picnics, or chats with local anglers. Just beware of mosquitos.

Be sure to stay for the sunset; it's the finest way to end your day on the Delta.

Boating is big business, so rentals are never a problem. Hundreds of marinas, resorts, and harbors are scattered throughout the area for your convenience. Herman and Helen's boat rental is an especially friendly, folksy spot serving locals as well as first-timers to the area. Even the river route mail carriers start and finish their 65-mile boat run there.

East and north via Highway 80 to 580 to 205, to Interstate 5 at Tracy heading towards Stockton. Turn left on "8 Mile Road" and follow it until it dead-ends at Herman and Helen's. Approximately 95 miles.

## 1–G    Canoe Cruising

Canoeing through the wilderness is a great one- , two- , or three-day adventure.

The gently flowing 60-mile Russian River in Sonoma County is one of the most popular for canoe-ing. It takes paddlers through rolling hills, orchards, mountain country, and beautiful redwood tree-lined banks at a leisurely pace.

Obviously all 60 miles from Cloverdale to Monte Rio can't be paddled in a single day. Bill Trowbridge of W. C. Trowbridge Canoe Trips has tips on different trips and the right canoes to take for them. His company has been in business for over 30 years and rents canoes for $19 a day (the price includes life jackets, paddles, and transportation back to your car). Canoes can also be rented on an hourly basis at some of the public beaches on the river.

The long hours under direct sun make T-shirts, sunscreen, hats, and sunglasses a must for these trips, so make sure you're well protected.

Canoers take to the Russian River in hordes during the summer months, so it's nice to take breaks along some of the empty sandy beaches. There is no food available along the river, of course, so bring a substantial picnic for your midday stop(s). After weekend trips, inexpensive barbecues are held from 4 P.M. to 7 P.M. at Healdsburg Veterans' Memorial Beach. To reserve a place at the barbecue and for further information on the canoe rentals, call Trowbridge at (707) 433-7247.

Country inns, cottages, and old roadhouses are tucked away all along the Russian River resort area. For a list of these and campgrounds, write or call the Russian River Visitor Information Center, 14034 Armstrong Woods Road, P.O. Box 331, Guerneville, California 95446, (707) 869-2584.

# 2—BIG ADVENTURES

Do you dare to windsurf on choppy waters or take a nose dive in a sailplane? Or raft in rougher waters? These are some of the big adventures Northern California has to offer. Try one of them and you'll probably find you're game for the rest.

## 2–A    Rolling with the River's Punches

Ten years ago the only river runners were hearty rough-and-tough outdoor types. Nowadays they include even those who have never even camped out.

In 1978 some 80,000 white-water rafters enjoyed the Stanislaus River on trips through the Stanislaus Canyon. But the 10-mile stretch of running rapids is in jeopardy; future rafters may not be able to enjoy the river's fast action and the canyon country of huge limestone cliffs, caves, and riverside woods. Unless the courts rule in California's favor in its suit against the United States government, the storage waters of the dam will drown the remaining stretch of Stanislaus rapids, turning it into a lake navigable only by motor-boats. A group called Friends of the River is fighting to give the stretch permanent protection, and rafters are enthusiastically supporting their efforts. River trips often end with participants writing letters to their local Congressional representatives.

Because the river's future is unknown (the filling of the reservoir behind the dam will be delayed until at least 1981), and because the canyon is so beautiful, the rafting trips have become increasingly popular.

The rapids demand total participation; the power of the water can be overwhelming. In between the roughest rapids—with names like Devil's Staircase and Widowmaker—there are quiet, peaceful stretches, magnificent cliffs and caves, swimming holes surrounded by smooth granite rocks, and huge fig trees. All make for excellent side trips and stopping points. Even though the 10-mile stretch can easily be completed in one day, a 2-day adventure complete with cookout and camping is more enjoyable. Why rush?

Either way, you'll get to know fellow paddlers and share good times. May and June are the months for those who relish the excitement of the roughest waters, while late summer is ideal for first-timers and families.

Several companies charter trips on the Stanislaus and other Northern California rivers (American, Tuolomne, Merced). One-day trips cost an average of $40—$50 per adult and 2-day outings run about twice as much. Meals and campsites are usually included—just bring your own sleeping bag, air mattress or pad, and eating utensils.

Call Friends of the River for the names of different touring companies and trips. Then phone well in advance (at least 2—3 months) for reservations, (415) 771-0400. There are various starting points for these trips, so get directions from the touring company you choose. It takes approximately 3 hours to reach the Stanislaus from San Francisco.

## 2–B    The Safest Form of Flying

That's what the folks at the Federal Aviation Administration call hot-air ballooning, and you'll believe it after sailing through the air with the greatest of ease. Airborn of Sonoma County is one of several companies that offer this fantastic-but-expensive early morning adventure (it costs $85 for the trip—which includes balloon and pilot). Flights take off early—7 A.M.—so balloons can get up and back down before the surface winds start up.

The 90-minute ride is so smooth that you'd never guess the balloon climbs at a rate of 200 feet per minute. We soon learned that watching our colorful balloon's shadow was the only way to see how fast we were moving.

Of course, there are other things to look at. As you cruise over several Sonoma towns you'll get a bird's-eye-view of rolling hills and mountain ranges. On a clear day you can see all the way out to the ocean. Even at a few thousand feet high you'll see towns wake up as cars and schoolbuses appear on the road and animals come out to pasture.

There's nothing quite like ballooning. According to Airborn pilot Christian Edelman, who's taken hundreds of trips, "Each flight is a challenge and different from all the others." Pilots are never sure exactly where they'll land, but passengers don't need to worry; the landing is every bit as smooth as the rest of the trip. We touched ground on Coast Guard property; others find themselves in parks or even someone's backyard. After landing, Airborn serves champagne for a festive ending to your morning adventure.

Call 4 to 6 weeks in advance to reserve for weekend flights, (707) 528-8133, or write Box 4887, Santa Rosa, California. North on U.S. 101 over the Golden Gate bridge. Take the Highway 12 exit toward Sonoma. Enter Sonoma County Fairgrounds on your right, where the trip begins. Approximately 55 miles.

## 2–C    Spelunking It

There are two ways to see the natural geological formations of Shasta caverns, located 800 feet above Lake Shasta. You can take a guided walking tour up stairs and through man-made tunnels and paved walkways, or you can crawl through the way it was done before these conveniences were developed.

Spelunking—cave exploration—definitely qualifies as a big adventure. It means getting down on your hands and knees for a good part of the trek; otherwise you'll never make it through tight tunnels and small closed-in areas.

You'll see fantastic crystalline stalactite and stalagmite formations, some of them a million years old. The caves are filled with the kind of intricate and graceful forms you might find in art museums and galleries, and stone "draperies" that look strangely like strips of bacon fill parts of the cave. The area at the top of the caverns is aptly named the Cathedral Room.

The first white explorer of the caverns left his mark more than 100 years ago, and it is still visible today. James A. Richardson, a federal fisheries employee taken into the caves by the Indians, signed his name and the date, November 3, 1878, with the carbide from his miner's lamp.

Spelunking isn't dangerous if you're in good physical condition and have the proper equipment. You'll need a hard hat with a chin strap and attached light, a flashlight, sturdy shoes, warm clothing that can be soiled or torn, gloves, kneepads, a change of clothing, and a canteen.

These special spelunking trips, for those over 14, are offered at 10 A.M. on Saturdays and Sundays. You will need advance reservations; write or call the Lake Shasta Caverns, P.O. Box 801, O'Brien, California 96070, (916) 238-2341. The cost is $10 per person.

The guided 2-hour tour, while not quite as exciting, is still one of the better mining tours in Northern California. It starts with a 15-minute boat cruise on Shasta Lake, followed by a bus trip up a winding road to the man-made entrance to the caves. The tour guides know what they're talking about, so it's unlikely you'll be able to stump them with any of your questions.

Open all year, with hourly trips from 8 A.M. on until dusk between May 1 and September 30. The winter schedule, from October 1 until April 30, offers three tours daily at 10 A.M., noon, and 6 P.M.

East and north via Highway 80 and Interstate 5 past Redding. Take the Shasta Caverns exit. Approximately 250 miles.

## 2–D    I Think I Can . . . I Think I Can

While enjoying the ocean and many other spectacular sights along a generally uncrowded Route 1, bicyclists not in the best of shape will huff and puff as they struggle to conquer the mostly uphill 35-mile trip north from Santa Cruz to Butano State Park.

En route, there are plenty of side trips and excuses for stopping. At the New Davenport store in Davenport, for instance, you'll find a fantastic collection of jewelry from all over the world and pottery from just around the corner. (Visitors can get directions to the Big Creek Pottery, then walk over to watch the potters at work.) If you need carbohydrates to burn off for the remainder of the trip, this is the place to fill up. The store/restaurant serves homegrown produce along with homemade soups, sandwiches, and pastries.

As invigorating as it feels to ride along the ocean, the turnoff east to Butano State Park means that the final few miles of your pedaling will be away from the wind and whatever traffic you encountered there. The road winds past meadows and hills to a 2200-acre park nestled in the Santa Cruz mountains. Even when the campsites are full during the busy summer season, bicyclists are never turned away; cycling is promoted as a means of travel.

From Butano back to Santa Cruz, the trip is a breeze. Going downhill with the wind at your back, you should sail home in two hours' time.

If you're not in shape for this ride, don't despair. There's a path for everyone in Santa Cruz, from the 100-mile-a-day cyclist to the weekend pedaler. Extensive routes are designated with signs on the road and pavement markings. You can pick up a free county bicycling guide at the County Governmental Center, the Public Library, or the County Convention and Visitors' Bureau.

For the Butano trip, any place you can park your car is fine for a starting point. If you don't bring your own bicycle with you, rent one at a cycling shop downtown.

## 2–E    Surfing with a Sail

You'll need courage, a body of water, a little wind, and about $60 for a couple of lessons to windsurf.

This is a relatively new sport started in California and has caught on worldwide. In the United States it is rapidly becoming a well-organized activity with competitive events scheduled year-round. Races, regattas, and clinics are held regularly for the estimated 15,000 windsurfers in this country.

The first windsurfing boat was designed in 1967 by Jim Drake, a California architect. He decided to build a boat that could easily be taken out during his lunch break, and the boats used for the sport today are essentially the same as his original model.

Windsurfers ride the waves on fiberglass boards about 12 feet long and 2 feet wide. They look like surfboards but are slightly larger. There's a mast, a boom, and a single sail to use for balancing. Most of the excitement comes from the speed you pick up as you sweep over the waters. The nose of the board will lift higher and higher as you move faster and faster.

You can learn the basics of windsurfing in about 6 hours. Several schools in the Bay Area offer lessons. Bay Surf Windsurfers in Foster City (in the Edgewater

Shopping Center) is the first windsurfing school in the country and the largest in the area. Call (415) 323-7257. Other schools include the Windsurfing Marina, Sausalito Marina, (415) 383-1226; the Berkeley Windsurfing School, Berkeley Marina, (415) 841-9463; Jack London Sports, 55 Alice Street, Oakland, (415) 444-5456, and Windsurf San Francisco, Pier 39, (415) 421-8353.

## 2—F     Toys in the Sky

Sailplanes may look like toys, but don't let that scare you. They are sturdy craft, and soaring is an exciting and safe travel adventure.

The Calistoga Soaring Center has been operating in the Napa Valley since 1968. For $32, a couple can take a scenic ride in one of these airplanes with a professional pilot, minus the propellers and jets. Gliders—the original name for sailplanes—have thin bodies, big wings, and a solitary wheel to balance them on the ground.

The secret to soaring lies in finding the air currents and riding them. Glider pilots follow the lead of hawks and buzzards. Once the plane is airborne and above the turbulent wind pockets, it's smooth sailing (flying?).

Your pilot can float you peacefully through the air, creating a strange sensation of weightlessness. If you want more adventure, your pilot might point the nose of the plane towards the sky, climb to a high altitude, and then do a nose dive straight toward the earth.

The landings are actually quite smooth as plane glides in, only inches off the ground, then skids to an easy stop.

The Calistoga Center is open 364 days a year from 9 A.M. until sunset. Fly in, or drive north and east via Highway 80 to 37 to 29 to Calistoga. Located at 1546 Lincoln Avenue, (707) 942-5592. Approximately 65 miles, a 90-minute drive.

Glider rides and instruction are also available at the Sky Sailing Airport in Fremont. East and south via Highway 80 and 17. Take the Durham Road exit west. Turn left at Christy Road, then go right onto a dirt road which leads directly to the airport. (415) 656-9900. Approximately 35 miles.

# 3—THINGS TO SEE AND DO ALONG THE OCEAN

The ocean can lure you to beachcombing, tidepooling, marinas and ports, to watch surfers and listen to the waves. Living near the ocean is not to be taken for granted. Millions of people in the Midwest rarely get to experience it, and only those on the West Coast can enjoy those extraordinary sunsets.

Beach weather is best between noon and late afternoon from September to the rainy winter season, and after the rains until the end of May. During the summer it's not unusual for the morning fog to hang on until midday. But whatever the weather, you can enjoy the beach year 'round.

## 3–A    Getting Wet and Digging Clams

The former isn't nearly as much fun as the latter, but even expert clam diggers have a difficult time staying dry. Wear high boots or old sneakers and bring along a change of clothing for this low-tide adventure.

There are clams to be found all along the mud flats in most Northern California bays, but if it's your first trip or you want guaranteed success, take a shovel and bucket to Lawson's Landing at Dillon's Beach in Marin.

After riding a barge out to the clamming grounds, the real fun starts as you walk and poke around the sand searching for holes the size of a quarter. When you suspect you've spotted one, start digging. Sometimes the clam can be 6 feet below the ground, so don't give up if you're not successful at first.

Clams come in all sizes and shapes. Gooeyducks are the quick large creatures, toughest to catch. Cockles are smaller and easily identifiable, as they resemble Shell Oil signs. Another variety, larger than the cockle, is the horseneck. Two gooeyducks, 10 horsenecks, and 50 cockles are the maximum you can collect.

You can have the rest of this adventure back at home, eating your catch. Let the clams soak first for several hours in a bucket of sea water.

To get to Dillon's Beach, drive north and west via U.S. 101 to Petaluma. Take Washington Street to the Bodega Highway exit through Tomales for 20 miles (Washington Street becomes Bodega Highway). The landing is 4 miles west of Tomales in the town of

Dillon's Beach. Approximately 65 miles; about 1½ hours with back country roads.

While it costs $2 for day use at the clamming grounds at Lawson's, other areas in Marin are free. They include Drakes Bay, Tomales Bay, Bodega Bay and the Bolinas Lagoon.

## 3–B    Combing California's Beaches

Northern California's beaches offer an abundance of treasures to those who know when and where to find them. And serious beachcombers know that early winter mornings after storms are the best time to search for exotic shells, pieces of driftwood, and glass balls from fishing nets—some even have Japanese imprints.

The beaches at the north end of Santa Cruz County, where Route 1 fronts the ocean, are a must for shell hunters. Snail shells, clam shells, abalone shells, and countless others abound on these stretches of sand.

No particular stretch of beach is best; just choose an area that hasn't already been scoured by other early risers. Driftwood seekers should look for places where rivers and streams meet the ocean.

State parks also welcome beachcombers, but you can't collect souvenirs. You'll have to throw back your findings for the next comer.

## 3–C    A Swimming Beach in Northern California?

There aren't many of these, unfortunately. But Stinson Beach Park in Marin has water warm enough for swimming and waves big enough for body surfing. The waters of Stinson, warmed by the sand banks of Bodega Bay, are frequented by hundreds of swimmers every day during the summer months. Weekends are especially crowded, with everyone intent on enjoying the sun and the water. There's terrific Frisbee action and even nonrunners can enjoy a jog on the beach. Children especially love the fine sand and can spend hours building dream castles.

Monarch butterflies arrive here during the winter (see 17-A), so Stinson is worth a visit even when it's too cold and dangerous to swim. The wildflower show every May is one of the best in the state.

North via Highway 101 to the Route 1 turnoff. Follow signs to Stinson. Approximately 18 miles.

## 3–D      Whale Watching Along the Coast

Almost any promontory along the coast of California makes a good place to watch for California grey whales as they migrate to their winter breeding grounds.

Almost 50 feet long and weighing over 90 tons, California grey whales are dark with patches of light grey and white. Their 5000-mile nonstop trip south— from the Arctic feeding grounds of Alaska's Bering Sea to the warm lagoons of Baja California for mating and calfbearing—takes these giant sea creatures within several miles of the shore between San Francisco and San Diego. Be sure to bring binoculars! Prime whale-watching areas in northern California are Point Reyes (see 15-F), Point Lobos (see 3-E), and Davenport, a hamlet 9 miles north of Santa Cruz. The best time for this is the month of January.

The whales usually travel in groups of 3 to 15, although it's not uncommon to spot one cruising alone. The huge mammals surface from a depth of 100 feet to blow or spout great blasts of warm air. Their blowholes are actually nostrils, which have moved up to the top of their heads through millennia of evolution. Occasionally these giant grey creatures hurtle themselves out of the water and then crash back into it, creating explosions of foam. This is called breeching.

Despite an international agreement made in 1938 to protect the California greys, several countries continue to talk of expanding whale-hunting operations to get oil from the mammals. Conservationists are acting to insure the whales' long-term survival.

Several organizations offer excursions between January and March. If you're interested in taking a 1- or 2-day voyage, call the Oceanic Society at (415) 441-4085, or Nature Expeditions International of Palo Alto at (415) 328-6572. Costs range from $8 to $30 depending on the length of your trip. The view from land is free.

## 3–E      Natural Outdoor Aquariums

All along the rocky headlands of the California coast there are tidepools to explore. Unfortunately, the future of tidepooling is in jeopardy because too many sea creatures have been taken out of their natural environments and left to die. So look but don't touch.

An enormous variety and concentration of marine life thrives in the Point Lobos area. At low tide the lovely water-filled pools among the rocks reveal colonies of colorful sea creatures. The more carefully you explore, the more you'll find in a few square feet of a tidepool. If you sit or stand quietly, you're sure to spot sea urchins, anemones, hermit crabs, and an assortment of plant and animal life. In the summer months there are two guided tours daily so you can learn more about who's who in the tidepools.

To get there via the most scenic route, take Highway 101 to 280 to Route 1 down the coast, 5 miles south of Carmel. $1 per car. Open daily 9 A.M. to 4 P.M. November through March, until 5 P.M. in April and October, 6 P.M. in May and June, and 7 P.M. in July and August. For more information call (707) 624-4909.

Another favorite place for tidepoolers is the rocky intertidal region adjacent to the Natural Bridges State Park in Santa Cruz. Each intertidal area supports unique marine life. Hermit crabs, shrimps, and sculpins live in the high deep pools, where a regular supply of fresh sea water keeps them alive. Sea lettuce, sea moss, and worms make their home in the "splash zone"—the only water they receive is from rain and splashes during high tides. Plant life is most abundant in the high exposed rock areas. Take Highway 101 to 280 to Route 1 heading south to reach Natural Bridges State Park. Approximately 72 miles.

## 3—F    Surfers and Sea Lions

If you want to watch surfriders gliding along the tops of waves or sea lions cavorting on giant rocks, Cliff House is the place to go.

The original Cliff House Bar and Restaurant was built on its present site overlooking the beach and rocks in 1863. That one burned down, as did several others. In another disaster in 1887, a schooner loaded with dynamite destroyed the Cliff House standing at that time. But the restaurant's name has never changed, and neither have the 200-foot cliffs that drop abruptly to level sandy beaches. The sunrises and sunsets you can see from here are spectacular.

Just a few feet from shore, directly below the Cliff House, is where the sea lions return to play year after year. If it's quiet you can hear them bark.

South of the restaurant the sandy beach extends non-stop for about 5 miles. Here, daring wetsuited surfers ride the waves at 20-25 miles per hour. It's a great spectator sport, and the surfers love the audience.

Late at night, when the tourist crowds have thinned, the bar at the Cliff House is a romantic and soothing place for a drink—especially if you can get a table by the ocean-front windows. During the day children can enjoy the lower floor of the Cliff House. It's filled with old coin-operated game machines, music boxes, and computerized pinball games.

The least direct but most glorious route to Cliff House is through Golden Gate Park. You can also rent a bicycle or roller skates on Stanyan or Fulton Street if you want a more leisurely way to get there. Take 101 to Fell-Laguna Streets exit. Follow Fell 20 blocks to entrance of Golden Gate Park.

## 3–G    Watching the Ships Sail By

San Francisco has one of the few deepwater landlocked harbors in the world. You can easily spend an entire day exploring the 6 miles along the waterfront. With a harbor guide map in hand (write to the San Francisco Port Commission, Ferry Building, San Francisco, California 94111 for a free map) you can go from one pier to the next watching fishermen make repairs, cars roll off ships, and passenger ocean liners depart for round-the-world voyages.

This port, called the Embarcadero ("landing place" in Spanish), dates back to the 1700s, when foreign trappers were taking cargoes of otter skins to China. But it did not really begin to flourish until the Gold Rush era.

Several master plan proposals for the waterfront are currently being studied. The Port Commission hopes to maintain a balance of maritime, commercial, and recreational use.

To explore the piers, start south of the ferry building at Piers 94 and 96. At the southeastern edge of the port near the Islais Creek Bridge, Pier 96 is unique because it has the only Lighter Aboard Ship (LASH) terminal on the West Coast. LASH terminals have the facilities to load and unload up to 500 tons of cargo from barges. Then go on to Piers 70 and 72, where you'll see foreign cars like Datsuns and Toyotas fresh off the boat.

Next stop is Bethleham Steel Shipyard, the largest ship repair in the Bay Area. You can get a close-up view of the action from the Mission Rock Restaurant and Bar. Sit on the outside deck for coffee, beer, or the fish fry on Friday nights. You'll be surrounded by fishermen and others who have discovered this unique place.

Piers 50, 48, and 46 are all good places to watch the ships sail by. Crown Zellerbach operates a paper terminal at Pier 48.

Sometimes called the coffee terminals, Piers 30 and 32 handle 28 percent of all coffee imported into the Bay

Area. Delta line ships also come in and leave from here every two weeks or so (check the business section of the *San Francisco Chronicle* or *Examiner* for schedules). The Delta line provides a unique combination of passenger and cargo service.

As you continue toward the ferry, you'll get a good view of the Bay Bridge. Right after you pass the ferry building you'll have your first opportunity to walk out on one of the long piers and check out the cargo handling facilities and shipping traffic.

The ferry building is the central point, and beyond this are the odd-numbered piers. Piers 15 and 17 are used exclusively for shipping newsprint and piers 27 and 29 are break-bulk facilities.

At Pier 35 you may be able to see a passenger ocean liner making a stop there along its route. In years past there were many more passenger ships than there are now. In fact, due to restrictions and regulations, you won't find any ships displaying an American flag. The Elizabeth II docked at Pier 35 last year for a break during its travels across the globe, and the Princess Cruises, English love boats, stop here periodically. Their arrival creates a real spectacle.

Piers 37, 39, and 41 are now known collectively as Pier 39. They were once used for foreign naval ships and now house restaurants, rides, and shops.

Other "special" ships arrive at Pier 45, near Fisherman's Wharf; last year a training ship for Coast Guard cadets docked here temporarily. The Wharf area is home for fishermen and fish processors; along with Ghirardelli Square and the Cannery, it's a famous city attraction.

## 3–H    Cruise Aboard a Boat

When you get tired of walking or driving and want to board a ship, you have several choices. From Pier 43½ in San Francisco, for example, you can take a 75-minute cruise of the Bay on the Red and White Fleet and see city landmarks along with the Bay Bridges. You'll sail by Alcatraz, the Presidio, and Treasure Island. Cruise ships depart every 30–45 minutes beginning at 10 A.M. The cost is $4.50, $4 for seniors, $2.50 for ages 5–11. No reservations are necessary. The cruises run daily, weather permitting. For more information call (415) 546-2810.

Swedish-designed Olson 31 sloops can be chartered for $7.50 per hour per person, or $190 a day for up to six people at Pier 39. Mike Krivohlavy, who arranges the trips, also gives private lessons. He's a licensed Coast Guard skipper. Phone him at (415) 661-6522.

Sam's Fishing Fleet will take you on a 45-minute cruise of Monterey Bay for $2, $1 for children 6–11. Another $2.50 gets you a fishing pole for your trip. Call (408) 372-0577 for information and directions.

If you've never been on a glass-bottom boat, go to the Lovers' Point Marina at 626 Ocean View Boulevard in Pacific Grove, just north of Monterey. For $2, $1.50 for children under 14, you'll see an abundance of marine life during this 30-minute cruise. Call (408) 372-2809.

Smaller sailboats can be rented at Aquatic Park in Berkeley. Typical rates are $3 an hour for an 8-foot boat, $8 an hour for a 14-foot heel boat, and $8 an hour for a 14-foot fast single-handed boat. Here you're on your own, so one of your crew must know how to sail. Call Gene Harris at (415) 548-3730 for reservations and further information.

# 4—BREATHTAKING VIEWS

If you're anywhere in Northern California, you're not far from a magnificent view. This is especially true of San Francisco. With its hills and steep streets, this city probably has more spectacular sights than any other. As you enjoy a panoramic view from one of the local vantage points, you're likely to feel both peaceful and exhilarated—and it's free.

## 4–A   Peek from the Peaks

On a clear day there's nothing like standing 910 feet above sea level on San Francisco's Twin Peaks, right in the center of the city. You'll have an all-encompassing view of the ocean, the Bay, and several Bay Area counties. The landmarks and geographical features that contribute to the splendor of San Francisco are easily definable. While visitors to the area search for the Golden Gate Bridge, the TransAmerica Pyramid, and the Palace of Fine Arts, residents can test their knowledge of the city by locating the streets and buildings where they live and work (Market Street, for example, is an easy find).

Take upper Market Street to Twin Peaks Boulevard. Start your sightseeing from the main observation area, then circle the road around the north and south peaks.

If it's foggy, and it often is, come back some other time. If it's windy, and it always is, stick around but wear a jacket.

## 4–B    Towering Above It All

Coit Tower, on Telegraph Hill, is the other popular lookout point in San Francisco. Getting there can be a problem, but it's worth the effort. Instead of driving up the narrow two-lane road and waiting for a parking space, you might park your car down below in the North Beach neighborhood and take a #39 Coit Tower bus from the Union and Columbus Streets intersection.

When you get to the parking area, resist the temptation to immediately take the elevator to the top of the tower, because the sweeping views you'll have from here are far more intoxicating than they are through the partitioned windows in the tower. The Embarcadero's docks and ships are directly beneath you, San

Francisco's crookedest street, Lombard, is just to the west, and many other impressive sights surround you.

The Mural Room in the base of the tower offers some exciting views as well. Colorful, lively portraits of life in the city during the 1920s and 30s fill the walls.

Built in 1934, Coit Tower was named after a San Francisco character, Lillie Hitchcock Coit, well known for chasing firefighters to the scene. She bequeathed funds to the city for its construction, and in fact some see its resemblance to a fire nozzle.

The tower is dramatically well-lit at night. After dinner in one of the great Italian restaurants in the neighborhood, a trip to the tower for a look at the dazzling lights below is better than any nightcap you could order—and cheaper.

You can ride the elevator to the top of the tower between 9 A.M. and 4:30 P.M. daily. The mural room is open from 2 to 4 P.M., with guided tours on Saturdays at 11 A.M.

## 4–C    A Different Kind of View

You don't have to ride an elevator to the top of a highrise or climb a mountain for a fascinating view.

Looking at a scale model that shows the interaction of sea water and fresh water along with the action of the tides can be equally spectacular.

Such a model was designed by the United States Army Corps of Engineers. It covers approximately 1½ acres of a Sausalito warehouse. The model is a hydraulic scale that simulates the tides and currents of the entire San Francisco Bay, a portion of the Pacific Ocean, and the Sacramento-San Joaquin Delta.

When the machinery is turned on, a 24-hour day passes in just 14.4 minutes, a year in 3½ days. For this reason Bay Area administrators and businesses use the model to study proposed changes in the waterway systems.

Don't plan to make a trip here unless the model will be in operation which is usually once every week or 10 days. Allow an hour and a half for a group tour, or wander through at your own pace with the self-guided recorded tours.

Open Monday through Friday and the first and third Saturdays of the month. Free. (415) 332-3870.

North via U.S. 101 to the Sausalito exit. Follow the road through Sausalito along the waterfront until you reach 2100 Bridgeway. Approximately 7 miles.

## 4—D    Village with a View

Even before you get to Sausalito, you'll be treated en route to glimpses of this town reminiscent of villages on the Italian and French Rivieras. Sausalito has retained this quality despite its popularity.

Take the Alexander exit which is the first one you'll reach after crossing the Golden Gate Bridge. As the road winds down into Sausalito you'll enjoy the views from both windows. You'll see Angel Island (see 16-A), Raccoon Straits, and, in the distance, San Francisco's skyline. On the other side you'll have your first look at some spectacular homes tucked into the hillside. (The prices are every bit as spectacular as the views.)

As the road levels off, it turns and becomes Bridgeway, Sausalito's main street. You'll find dozens of unusual small shops and fine restaurants along the waterfront here. The Trident Restaurant, open Tuesday through Sunday from 11 A.M. until 2 A.M., serves unique dishes. You can also enjoy the decor and the view from the outside deck behind the restaurant.

Further south on Bridgeway is the Village Fair, a mini-Ghirardelli Square area reminiscent of Lombard

Street. Tourists can delight in the maze of specialty shops here.

The food at the Alta Mira Hotel doesn't get the rave reviews it did ten years ago, but the sweeping views from its deck are still the best in town. To get to the Alta Mira, at 126 Harrison Avenue, climb up the stairs near the Village Fair on Bridgeway. The restaurant is open from 8 A.M. until 9 P.M.

Parking is a problem in Sausalito, so you should consider using the Golden Gate Transit bus service. Call (415) 332-6600. If you take the bus, you can get off at the Golden Gate Bridge to take in the sights and, if you like, walk across the bridge and board a bus on the Marin side. Your other option is the Golden Gate Ferry. Call (415) 332-6660 for schedules and price information.

## 4-E   Thirty-Five Counties Come into View

Mount Diablo is the highest point in the Bay Area, and on a clear day you can see as many as 35 of the state's 58 counties. That's 80,000 square miles of land and sea, including the Sierras and the Central Valley's waterways.

The summit—elevation 3849 feet—is usually bathed in sunshine, even on overcast days. Occasionally in winter the peak gets a light coat of snow.

In the 18th century Mount Diablo served as a reference point for Spanish explorers and early California settlers. Since 1851 it has been the survey control point for Northern and Central California.

On a weekday in February, you'll probably have the place to yourself. Take advantage of the park's facilities for hiking and picnicking. Camping sites are also available.

East and south via Highway 80 to 580 to 24. Take Interstate 680 until you reach Danville, then follow signs to Mount Diablo. The winding mountain road up to the mountain's peak provides excellent views. Approximately 30 miles.

## 4–F   Where Mountains Meet the Sea

Nepenthe, named for the mythical drug that made people forget their sorrows, is indeed magical. The sweeping views and peace of mind you'll have when you see it will tell you why.

In Big Sur County, 800 feet above sea level, Nepenthe is the name of a redwood pavilion designed by one of Frank Lloyd Wright's students. The original building was constructed in the 1940s as a honeymoon cottage for Rita Hayworth. Today Nepenthe is a restaurant and bar, and perfect stopping place along the dramatic 30-mile ocean drive from the Carmel-Monterey area. It is also a social and cultural center.

Nowhere are the views of the southern Big Sur region and massive rugged coastline more spectacular. Stand on the outside terrace to enjoy the fresh air and the view.

Nepenthe's simple natural structures enhance rather than disturb the harmony of its setting. The visual pleasure and spiritual peace it offers and its selection of fine foods make it a unique and satisfying experience. Open every day at noon, and usually open until midnight. Call (408) 667-2345.

Drive south on U.S. 101 to 152 to Route 1. In Big Sur County look for the sign to Nepenthe. (Be sure to stop at a few of the scenic turnouts between Monterey and Nepenthe.) Approximately 145 miles.

## 4–G    The Bay from Berkeley

One of the best views of the San Francisco Bay Area is a panorama that includes the city itself along with most of the University of California and the town of Berkeley.

As you take Highway 80 toward Berkeley, look east toward the hills just after crossing the Bay Bridge. Way on top, you'll see a huge grey building, the Lawrence Hall of Science, where you're headed. The trip up to the museum is quite scenic when it begins to travel the crest of the East Bay hills.

From the museum, you'll be surprised to discover how flat Berkeley really is. After taking in all the sights outside and exploring some of the trails, you may want to look at the gadgets in the museum.

Inside and outside, the Lawrence Hall of Science shouldn't be missed. East and north via Highway 80 to 17 to University Avenue exit. Take University up towards campus. Turn left at Oxford, then take your first right onto Hearst. Another right onto Gayley, a left on Rimway, and a left on Centennial to the top of the hill. Approximately 15 miles.

# 5—BIRD WATCHING

You don't need money or expertise to bird watch. The popularity of this activity has soared during the last 10 years, and an estimated 2 million people presently take part in birding activities throughout the country. Most of them are not experts—they don't have to be. To learn the names of all the strange and wonderful birds, you can purchase a copy of the *Field Guide to Western Birds* or seek out the expert at the spot you've chosen for your birding activities.

All of the places listed below are free and scenic.

## 5—A   You'd Regret Not Seeing an Egret

To see egrets sailing through wooded groves or touching bills with their mates, you can take a trip to the Audobon Canyon Ranch in Marin County.

An easy quarter-mile climb through woodlands and wildflowers takes visitors to the main observation area. You'll be able to see stunning white egrets and great blue herons nesting in the tops of imposing redwoods.

By May, several eggs have hatched; peering through the powerful telescopes affords you a close-up view of the birds' family life. (If you want to watch the action without worrying about the next person in line, bring along your own set of binoculars.) But you won't need binoculars to hear the harsh calls of the heron or the quieter sounds of the egret.

Classes and lectures are held for visitors interested in finding out more about these birds. Call (415) 383-1044 to register in advance. You might also like to wander inside the big white ranch house at Audobon Canyon. There you'll see photography exhibits and charts detailing the life cycles of the egret and heron. After observing the bird life in the canyon, many visitors enjoy a picnic on the property.

Open Saturdays, Sundays, and holidays between March and July (the nesting season), 10 to 4. Contribution requested.

North via U.S. 101 and Highway 1, 3 miles north of Stinson Beach. Follow signs. Approximately 15 miles.

## 5—B   Wild Water Birds

At Lake Merritt in Oakland, five small man-made islands are the nesting sites for egrets, herons, and waterfowl from as far away as Alaska and Siberia. You'll see wild species of birds like Canadian and white Frontier geese, a mixed flock of ducks that includes green-headed mallards, and, in the winter, some wild and unusual diving ducks that migrate here for a season.

The wild ducks and geese are so used to being around people that the park rangers allow visitors to join them in their daily 3:30 feedings. The rangers are also available to answer questions and give bird-identification lectures to interested groups. They'll direct you to the area behind the snack bar if you want to see some injured native California birds that need caging, or to the Rotary Natural Science Center, which houses hawks and owls.

Lake Merritt is the largest salt water lake in the world completely contained in one city. After birdwatching, you may want to rent a boat, or walk or drive around the surrounding area. (415) 273-3091.

East and south via Highway 80 and 580 to the Grand Avenue exit. Take Grand a quarter of a mile to Bellevue Street, where you'll see the entrance. Approximately 15 miles.

## 5—C    Kites You Can't Fly

At the Coyote Hills Regional Park in Fremont, you can watch white-tailed kites as they hover in a single spot, then swoop to the ground in search of mice and other rodents. Unlike other birds of prey, the kites can maintain their position in the air without moving forward for long periods of time.

This 1000-acre park, filled with fresh- and saltwater marshes, has wooden ramps to walk on just above the water level (or a 3½-mile paved path to bicycle on). You'll see a fine assortment of both land birds and water fowl, and a variety of interpretive programs and tours are scheduled. For reservations and further information call (415) 471-4967.

Just north of the park, there's an 11½-mile creek trail. Bikers, hikers, and equestrians can go east about 9 miles into Niles Canyon, or west for 2½ miles to the Bay. (If you cycle late in the afternoon, travel toward the canyon so the wind will be riding with you.) The path is level, so you should be able to save most of your energy for watching the birds and other sights.

The park is open from 8 A.M. until sundown. Parking costs $1 per vehicle per day. Take Highway 80 to 17 south to Jarvis Street west offramp. Go about 1 mile until you reach Newark Boulevard. Turn right, then go left on Patterson Road after about a mile. Approximately 25 miles.

## 5–D     More Than 300 Species of Birds

The Point Reyes Peninsula is one of the most abundant bird areas in the United States. It's a great place to see some rare and unusual land birds.

Your first stop should be at the Point Reyes park headquarters in Olema to pick up bird maps and checklists, so you can learn about the many varieties of birds in Marin and where to locate them.

In the wee hours of morning, you can watch the observatory staff netting and banding birds at the Palomarin Beach on Mesa Road at the southern tip of Point Reyes (ask at park headquarters for directions). Each caught bird gets a unique band with its own number; the bands are used to monitor how well they are doing and where they migrate to and from. This national program has bird-banding labs in several regions of the country. Call ahead of time to find out which mornings the banding occurs and the exact times, (415) 868-1221.

The Mendoza and Abandoned Ranches are two of many other lookout points in Point Reyes where you can see rare land birds like warblers. Get a Point Reyes map to find the exact location of these places.

Fall is the best time to find the migrating birds; in the winter you'll see the greatest variety of shore and water birds.

# 6—LITTLE OLD TOWNS AND LITTLE OLD STORES

The populations of Northern California's country towns range in size from 100 to 1000. Their main streets usually have a general store, where the clerks know most people in town by their first names, a saloon or two, a restaurant, often a hotel, and always a post office.

These towns are rich in history. Many of the old buildings date back to the mid-19th century. It's not hard to find someone with stories to tell about the old days. There are no long lines in these places at the bank, the post office, or the gas station. Your visit will give you an enjoyable taste of small-town life and its pleasures.

## 6—A    The Best Breakfasts in the Gold Country

Volcano was once one of the largest towns in California. Nearly 50,000 people lived here in the 1850s when the town had 17 hotels, a score of brothels, a library, several theaters, and a court of quick justice.

About 100 people live here today. Volcano is a close-knit community where everyone in town has Christmas dinner together and where there are nearly as many dogs as there are people.

Many of the old buildings, or their ruins, are still here, and each one is identified by a hand-painted plaque. The old Eagle Bandstand is now a gift shop and the Assay Office is a bookstore. The general store has been in continuous use since 1852, and next to it is an artisan's gallery run by local artist Brad Devereaux. The old Union Hotel Billiards Saloon and Boarding House, once famous for its "large and delicious meals" and now famous for its ghosts, is the home and studio of potter Rod Hanchett.

Volcano may be small, but the weekends are as lively today as they were in the old days. It could be a Volcano Pioneer Players production or the St. George Hotel that brings people up here. Or it might be the Jug and Rose Restaurant, serving the best breakfasts you'll ever have in the Gold Country.

From California 49 take California 88 east at Jackson. Make a left at the Volcano-Pine Grove Road turnoff. Volcano is 2 miles past the Chaw-Se Indian Grinding Rocks State Park.

Lodging at the St. George Hotel, P.O. Box 275, Volcano, California 95689, telephone (209) 296-4448.

Nearby camping at the Chaw-Se Indian Grinding Rocks State Park, 2 miles southwest of Volcano on Volcano-Pine Grove Road.

Breakfast at the Jug and Rose, Main Street, Volcano, telephone (209) 296-4696. Call a day in advance for reservations. Approximately 140 miles.

## 6—B    Stop for a Drink in an Old Saloon

When pioneer merchant George Coulter opened up a tent business for miners in 1850, he had no idea that the site of his business would be named after him four years later. By the mid 1850s Coulterville, as it was then called, was the center of rich placer mines in the southern Motherlode. The mines had names like Maxwell, Boneyard, and Black Creek.

Today Coulterville is the second largest town in Mariposa County (Mariposa is the largest), but it looks much like it did in the mining days. Located at the intersection of California Highways 49 and 132, it's a good place to spend an hour or so on your way to Yosemite from the Bay Area via California 132. (Possibly this route is more scenic than the heavily used California 120–108.)

Most of the old buildings on Main Street are still standing. The newest building in town, in fact, is the Union gas station and general store (built shortly after World War II), where you can get your car's "minor mechanical problems solved" and a cold beer or some ice cream for yourself (temperatures can run into the high 80s here through mid-October).

The Jeffrey Hotel was in continuous use for over 129 years until it was sold in late 1979. The old Knights of Pythias Hall and General Store is now an antique and "Americana" store. There are still a couple of old-time saloons open where you can learn about the old days from some of the last surviving prospectors in the mining country.

From Interstate 580 take California 132 east until it intersects California 49 at Coulterville. Yosemite National Park is 30 minutes away via County Road J20 and California 120. Approximately 140 miles.

## 6—C    Joaquin Murrieta Began His Career Here

Up California 4 from Angels Camp is the town of Murphys, a natural stopping place on your way to visit the Calaveras Big Trees. Named for its founders, John and Daniel Murphy, it started as a trading post in 1848. After gold was discovered here a year later, Murphys grew into one of California's principal mining towns. It was here that the bandit Joaquin Murrieta began his murderous career. Legend has it that over $20 million worth of gold (in 19th-century prices) came out of Murphys Flat and the surrounding mines.

Today Murphys is one of the most beautiful towns in the Motherlode. Gingerbread Victorian houses and tall locust trees line the streets. Most of the old buildings are still here, although a fire destroyed much of the business section in 1859. Down Main Street you can still stay at the old Murphys Hotel Saloon and Restaurant, dating back to 1856. Dr. Jones's Apothecary Shop is now an antique store. The Old Timer's Museum (25¢ for adults, children free) displays artifacts of the old days. Just outside town, Murphys Grammar School, built in 1860, is one of the oldest schoolhouses still in use in California.

From California 49 at Angels Camp, take California 4 east about 8 miles.

Food and lodging at Murphys Hotel Saloon and Restaurant, P.O. Box 329, Murphys, California 95247, telephone (209) 728-3454. Approximately 140 miles.

## 6—D    Center of the Placer Mining Country

Mokelumne Hill is a town untouched by the 20th century. The name comes from an Indian word for the nearby river. The earliest white settlers here were French trappers. After gold was discovered in the area in 1848, Mokelumne Hill became the center of placer mining in Calaveras County.

Just 8 miles south of Jackson on California 49, "Moke Hill" is a good place to spend a few hours some afternoon. The old Hotel Leger, a relic of the gold mining days, still operates a saloon and restaurant daily. There's an ice cream shop just down the street, and an antique and crafts store across the way. The old International Order of Odd Fellows (I.O.O.F.) Building is now the town library. And the town hall at the south end of town, built in 1900, is still the center for Moke Hill's many social, political, and cultural events.

From California 49 take the Mokelumne Hill "Historic Loop" exit 8 miles south of Jackson.

Food and lodging at Hotel Leger, P.O. Box 50, Mokelumne Hill, California 95245, telephone (209) 286-1401. Approximately 140 miles.

## 6—E    Locke Still Looks the Same

Visitors to Locke, an authentic Chinese community in the Delta country, will feel as though they're traveling into the past.

Founded in 1912, Locke looks now very much as it did then. The original buildings—all Chinese architecture—still stand; the new housing tract developments and condominiums that have destroyed other ethnic neighborhoods have not yet invaded this area. State Assemblyman Art Agnos hopes to keep it that way, and he's working behind the scenes to insure the continued preservation of this historic community.

Locke's residents contributed to the development of levees in the Sacramento Delta. At one time the town bustled with a theater, post office, bakery, six restaurants, and nine grocery stores to serve a population of 1500.

Today only about 100 people call Locke home, and most of the businesses and shops have closed down. One restaurant whose doors remain open to locals and tourists is Al's Place. Ever since 1934 Al's has been serving sizzling steak dinners. The ceiling is decorated with $1 bills donated by patrons who want to see how the bartender manages to put them there. Even if you aren't hungry, stop in at Al's for a drink and a little local gossip. You're sure to hear a good tale or two.

One building was recently converted into a small museum with displays that tell the story of Locke. Don't miss it.

Take Highway 80 to 580 to 205 to Interstate 5 to Highway 113. Approximately 105 miles. You can combine this visit with your trip to the Sacramento Delta.

## 6—F    A Portuguese Community Thrives Here

About a thousand people live and work in Pescadero, a thriving Portuguese community less than 70 miles from the heart of San Francisco. A visit here is like taking a trip across space and time.

Duarte's Restaurant on Stage Road serves up home-cooked dishes at old-time prices (soup, salad, bread and butter, filet of sole, apple pie, and coffee for under $5!). Duarte's also uses the area's abundant artichokes in delicious thick soups and omelets.

Down the block from Duarte's, Molly Ramolla will gladly give you a personal tour of her studio exhibit and explain the work that went into her unusual handmade papyrus paintings and prints.

Locals gather at the Williamson General Store, the best place for picking up information about this colorful town and people. Browse here and enjoy yourself, and don't leave without talking to some of the locals.

May is the best month to visit Pescadero, when the Portuguese community takes to the streets en masse for the Chamarita Festival of the Holy Ghost (see the May listings in Chapter 23). After the parade everyone is welcome to a free barbecue.

Take U.S. 101 south to Interstate 280 to California 1 to Pescadero Road, then go two miles inland. Approximately 65 miles.

# 7—UNUSUAL MUSEUMS

Northern California offers an outstanding group of museums. The major Bay Area museums—the San Francisco Metropolitan Museum of Art, the Oakland Museum, the M. H. de Young Memorial Museum, and the Palace of the Legion of Honor in San Francisco—usually top visitors' lists. But the smaller, lesser-known places are also worthy of exploration. Their assorted collections include trains, dolls, and radio equipment. Whatever your hobby or interest, there's probably a museum you'll enjoy.

## 7–A    A Voyage into the Past

You'll feel you've actually been there when you climb aboard the *C. A. Thayer* at San Francisco's Maritime Historic Park and learn about its history. The *Thayer,* a three-masted wood-hulled schooner, was built in 1895 and used primarily to carry lumber. Here you can explore the crew's living quarters while a magic wand tells their stories. A special sound system provides information about life on the ships whenever you come within range of the sound fields scattered throughout the museum—kids love it.

Next walk through the passenger section of an even bigger ship, the *Wampona*. Also built in 1895, the *Wampona* traveled between the state's ports.

Before the Bay Bridges were constructed, the *Eureka* carried passengers and their vehicles to and from the city. This last of the paddle-wheel ferries was powered by a 12-foot stoke steam engine which turned 27-foot paddlewheels. Even today there are several antique cars and trucks on the ship's lower deck. Upstairs you can put another nickel in the nickelodeon (it costs a quarter now) and dance to some oldies but goodies.

These three ships, along with two recent additions to the fleet, are constantly being restored. Don't hesitate to watch or ask questions. At the entrance to the park there's a small store that displays contemporary seamen's instruments. Located near Fisherman's Wharf, Ghirardelli, and the Cannery, the park is open from 10 A.M. to 6 P.M. daily (10 to 5 between October and April), and it's free.

If you're not yet seasick, take a short walk to the *Balclutha*, an old square-rigger that sailed around Cape Horn 17 times. You're welcome to walk the decks of this floating museum of the Gold Rush era.

## 7–B    Transit History Kept Alive

The trains at the California Railway Museum in Sonoma County won't take you from one town to another, but you can board renovated old-time railroad cars to travel across this 23-acre outdoor spectacle.

This unusual museum is operated by a nonprofit organization for the preservation and protection of historic vehicles. It features the largest variety of operating railway locomotives and cars in the western United States. The 70-piece collection includes steam-diesel and electric locomotives, freight and passenger cars, street cars, interurbans, el cars, and work equipment.

You can explore the Sacramento Northern Interurban car that transported rail passengers between 1914 and 1941, a New York elevated train that served in California during World War II, and a Pullman train complete with a berth made up for the night.

Volunteer members of the Bay Area Electric Railroad Association will probably be busy painting and making repairs while you're there. But they're never too busy to talk about the history of the museum and how they acquired the old trolleys and locomotives, or their theories about transportation of the future.

Train rides through the property cost $1.50 for adults, 75¢ for children.

Open noon to 5 P.M. holidays, weekends, and daily during summer months.

East on Highway 80 to State Highway 12, then 11 miles on 12 to Rio Vista Junction, where the California Railway Museum is located. Approximately 50 miles.

## 7–C    Fascination of the Firemen

The Firemen's Pioneer Museum is a must for kids— even those who generally shy away from "cultural" trips. The museum is actually in one of San Francisco's fire stations, and if the fire fighters aren't out on an emergency call, they'll give a special greeting to the kids and talk about their work.

Until recently, on-duty fire fighters took turns giving the hour-long tours, but too often an alarm would end the visits abruptly and sometimes delay the fire fighters. Now that the effects of Proposition 13 are being felt throughout the fire department, several San Francisco stations have had to shut down.

The tours continue, however, and enthusiastic city volunteer guides now show off old fire memorabilia. You'll see hand-drawn pumps, water grenades, antique uniforms, and the photograph displays lining the walls of the station.

Children can sit behind the wheel of an ancient fire truck and ring the bells on the engines (guides report that this seems to be *everyone's* favorite part of the tour).

The free museum is open Thursday through Sunday from 1 P.M. to 4 P.M. It's located at 655 Presidio Street at the Pine Street intersection.

## 7–D    Thank You, Walter Johnson

Walter Johnson is the man who donated $2 million in 1967 to restore the Palace of Fine Arts to all its past splendor. Originally built to house the fine arts exhibit of the Panama Pacific International Exhibition in 1915, the Palace now has a 20th-century museum called the Exploratorium. It specializes in science technology and human perception, and there's always something exciting to see. The broad collection of over 200 exhibits is designed to make you more conscious of your perceptual powers. The attractions include an aluminum foil strobe-lit room, a musical instrument played by solar energy and two-dimensional pictures that look three-dimensional. Stop, look, listen, and touch so you can solve some of these mysteries. The exhibits demand participation.

The outside of the Palace, which resembles a Roman ruin, is equally magical. There's a small lagoon with ducks and swans right on the property, and at night the Palace is one of the most romantic places in San Francisco.

In October the San Francisco International Film Festival is held here, and other concerts are scheduled throughout the year.

The museum has recently been renovated, so call (415) 563-7337 to find out its new hours. There is no charge, but donations are encouraged.

The Palace of Fine Arts is located at 3601 Lyons Street at Lombard Boulevard in the Marina neighborhood.

## 7–E    A Doll's House

There used to be horses in the stalls of this old green-and-white barn in Bodega. Now the place teems with an international cast of characters: dolls from all over the world.

Ranging from a half an inch in height to life size, the dolls and mannequins in Charlene's Yesterday Museum are totally enchanting. These dolls, from all over the world and many a century old, are made from papier mâché, wax, china, wood, and cloth. Charlene has been collecting them for some 20 years now.

One stall looks like a turn-of-the-century schoolroom; another transports visitors to Grandma's country kitchen, complete with a 1902 stove and 1925 washer. The foreign dolls live in the hayloft of the barn, and they have a special miniature chapel with stained glass windows.

If Charlene's home looks familiar, you probably recognize it from Alfred Hitchcock's eerie movie, *The Birds*. The house was one of several in the area used in the film. Visitors are invited to see the display Wednesday through Sunday between 11 A.M. and 5 P.M. (she suggests calling first to make sure she's not out on an errand). The cost is 50¢ for adults, 25¢ for children.

North via U.S. 101 past Petaluma. Take the second Rohnert Park exit and turn left at the stop sign toward Sebastopol. Go 5 miles or so until you can make a left onto Bodega Highway. Follow for 8 miles until you reach the town of Bodega, then look for the green-and-white building with a flag in front of it. Call first (707) 876-3282. Approximately 45 miles.

## 7-F    Mural, Mural on the Wall

You can trace the entire history of the U.S. Navy and Marine Corps on a huge mural covering one whole side of the Navy Marine Museum on Treasure Island.

This building, which houses the museum, served as the Administration office for the Golden Gate International Expo of 1939. The museum project was developed solely for the bicentennial celebration, but has since become a permanent collection depicting events from 1813 to the present.

In conjunction with the mural there are displays and exhibits. Huge intricate models of the Navy vessels used to explore the Pacific, dismantled lights from California's lighthouses, and spacecraft models comprise the varied collection along with more typical items such as flags, uniforms, and weapons.

The museum is free and open daily from 10 A.M. to 3:30 P.M.

East on Highway 80 halfway over the Bay Bridge. Check out the view as you exit on the Treasure Island turnoff and drive through Yerba Buena Island to the museum. Approximately 8 miles.

## 7-G    They Were Here First

Long before the white man arrived, California was home to numerous Indian tribes. The State Indian Museum in Sacramento offers a unique glimpse of their cultures.

The display includes tribal clothing, jewelry and musical instruments. You'll also see pottery, basketry, and featherwork. Learn about rituals and ceremonies like the ghost dance of the Sioux and Cheyenne.

The exhibits, which change often, range from mythology to archaeology. Photographs of the Indians at daily tasks—building fires and skinning animals—recreate scenes from long ago.

The Indian Museum is right next to Sutter's Fort, a great place to escape into California's history. Both are open daily, except holidays, from 10 A.M. to 5 P.M., with a 25¢ charge for adults.

Located at 2618 K Street in Sacramento. Take Highway 80 east to the downtown Sacramento exit. Follow the alphabet to K Street. Approximately 88 miles.

## 7–H    Over and Out

Radio enthusiasts will delight in exploring the broad collection of ancient radio tubes, spark transmitters, receivers, and klytrons on display at the Foothill College Electronics Museum.

Even those unfamiliar with the workings of radios and sound wave transmission will be intrigued by some of the special exhibits that allow visitors to experiment with the equipment.

Open Wednesday and Thursday 9 A.M. to 5 P.M., Friday 9 A.M. to 10 P.M., and weekends 1 P.M. to 5 P.M. Closed during the summer. Go south on U.S. 101 to 280 to the Foothill College exit. You may want to see the planetarium here, too. Approximately 40 miles.

## 7–I    No "Hands Off" Signs Here

After visiting the Lawrence Hall of Science at U.C. Berkeley, you'll wish more of your school studies had taken place outside the classroom.

Lawrence was built in 1968 as a research facility for science education. The exhibits and displays invite visitors to explore the worlds of biology, chemistry, math, astronomy, and computer science. The museum is filled with sophisticated computers and electronic equipment.

Do-it-yourself gadgets test your knowledge of assorted subjects. On weekends the Biology lab and telescope area are open.

Open 10 A.M. to 5 P.M. weekdays, except 10 A.M. to 9 P.M. Thursday. Open 10 A.M. to 4:30 P.M. on weekends. $1.75 for adults, 75¢ for seniors, students, and those under 18 years old.

For directions see 4-F.

## 7–J    Look Through a Telescope

As you approach Lick Observatory, at the top of Mount Hamilton in the Diablo mountain range, sprawling San Jose will look like a toy town far below. The observatory is reached by a pleasant drive from U.S. 101 with magnificent views over the valley.

There are eight telescopes at Lick, which is operated by the University of California. One of the buildings (which looks like a silver blister from the freeway below) houses a 120-inch optical telescope. You'll see this giant from a glassed-in balcony. The telescope weighs 145 tons but is so perfectly balanced that it can be moved by a 1/25 horsepower motor.

Perhaps the most famous telescope, though, is the

36-incher. While the 120-incher is a mirror reflector, this one is a refractor. You look through a lens just as with binoculars. The surrounding floor can be raised as much as 16½ feet so the observer can look very comfortably into the eyepiece. Second to arrive on the mountain, this telescope has been in constant use since the turn of the century and is still doing valuable work. There are guided tours of this telescope from 1:00 to 5:00 P.M. daily.

On Friday evenings from July to mid-September, the telescope is available for public viewing. First there's a lecture by an astronomer, then the telescope is aimed at a selected celestial body. Tickets for this lecture and viewing are scarce, and it is suggested that you apply as early as April to the Summer Visitor's Program, Lick Observatory, Mount Hamilton, California 95140. Give a first and second choice of dates, preferably a few weeks apart. There is a limit of 6 tickets per request.

The gallery is open from 10:00 A.M. to 5:00 P.M. daily except Thanksgiving, Christmas, and University of California holidays.

Take the Alum Rock offramp from U.S. 101 at San Jose and go east, then go right on Mount Hamilton Road. Approximately 22½ miles from the freeway, 70 miles from San Francisco.

# 8—HARVEST TIME

California boasts the world capitals of artichokes, apricots, avocados, grapes, raisins, peaches, plums, prunes, garlic, lemons, olives, dates, almonds, and walnuts. And of course you can find practically every other fruit and vegetable in abundance here too.

There's no reason to limit these items to what you find in the neighborhood supermarket. Hundreds of California's farmers sell their home-grown produce directly to the public, and many even let you pick your own crop. You'll get quality, freshness, and a great bargain. Besides, you'll have a lot more fun out in the fields with your family and friends than you will going up and down the aisles by yourself.

A directory listing more than 450 direct-sale farmers includes information on canning, harvest dates, and nutritional values. It can be obtained free by calling the Farmer-Consumer Information Line (800) 952-5272.

## 8–A    All in the Family . . . Farm

Name your favorite kind of apple—Red Delicious, Golden Delicious, Newton Pippin, McIntosh, Jonathan, Prime Gold. Whatever your pleasure, you'll find it at one of the family farms in Pajaro Valley just east of Watsonville. Chances are you'll also find apples rarely available in the supermarket, and some you never heard of before.

The annual apple harvest starts in early September and lasts through December. Splendid country roads wind through hills, orchards, and redwoods, past lakes and old ranches to orchards and the strong smell of ripening fruit.

The Gizdich family has been in the apple business for over 40 years. Mom, Dad, Grandma, and two boys all work on the ranch. When they first started selling directly to the public 15 years ago, all the sorting and polishing was done by hand. Today these processes are mechanized. Apples are sold by the box in a new red barn where all varieties are displayed for tasting. Or, if you prefer, you can go into the fields and do your own picking. Containers can be rented for 15¢.

In the apple-sorting shed, apple juice is made in a blend-as-you-taste operation on Saturday mornings. While rock music plays in the background, a sampler tests the juice and calls for a new variety of apples when the mixture gets too sweet. The formula constantly changes as the season progresses and the apples get sweeter.

Take 101 south to State Highway 152 in Gilroy. The descent from Mount Madonna County Park provides sweeping views of the valley (on clear days you can see the ocean). Right after 152 levels off, you'll see a sign: "Apples: Farmer to You." The next few signs on Carlton Road will take you to the Gizdich ranch. (408) 722-1056. Approximately 68 miles.

## 8–B    Perfect Apricots

Perfect apricots are one of four kinds of fruit harvested at the Three Nunns farm in Brentwood. They are also called Brentwood Gems, and when you bite into the soft orange fruit you'll know why.

The Three Nunns farm is owned and operated by the Three Nunns—George, Ron, and Jane. Their father supplied apricots and peaches to the canneries in the 1930s. In the following decade their mother started selling the fruit, grown in her backyard, directly to the public. Today most of the cannery sales have been phased out in favor of direct sales.

Apricot season is short, lasting all of three weeks. After the Perfects are harvested around June 10, Bleinheims are picked. These are the sweetest of the apricots. The Royals are next; these are best for canning. Last to be picked are the light-colored Tilton apricots.

The Nunns are good hosts and provide customers with buckets, ladders, containers, and boxes. They'll even give lessons and a free pamphlet on drying the fruits. In addition to apricots, their primary product, they also grow and sell cherries, strawberries, peaches, apples, and pears.

East and north via Highway 80 to 580 to 24 to 4, one mile past Brentwood. Approximately 55 miles.

## 8—C    Whew!

The Southern Santa Clara Valley calls itself the garlic capital of the world. Nearly 90 percent of the garlic consumed nationwide is produced here.

Last year growers, producers, and lovers of the "stinking rose" celebrated the summer harvest with a weekend festival. The festivities included a garlic rec-ipe contest, strolling minstrels, a Garlic Queen contest, and belly dancers. These were so successful that they are well on their way to becoming an annual event.

Garlic freaks can delight in such culinary delicacies as garlic- and parsley-stuffed mushrooms, garlic-steeped calamari, and scampi. (Don't worry, non-garlic eaters won't go hungry. Pepper steak sandwiches, tacos, and strawberry sundaes are also on the menu.)

In addition to all the eating, there are booths for browsing and buying items like garlic braids. You can also take tours of the garlic fields and processing plants.

The 1979 festival was held in the beginning of August. Call (408) 842-6437 for location and the exact schedule of events. The Santa Clara Valley is about 65 miles from San Francisco.

## 8—D    A Mixed Bag

Cherry picking in May starts the season at the German Ranch near Fairfield. During the summer months, vegetables like tomatoes, corn, black-eyed peas, and bell peppers are picked on one side of the field while peaches and pears lure fruit-lovers on the other.

For 35 years the German ranch, named after the original owners, has been growing dozens of fruits and vegetables. Today the Blythe family runs the ranch, which specializes in juicy tomatoes and peaches.

The fruit orchards have a permanent home but the vegetable crops rotate each year. According to Jack Blythe, general manager, "Different plants give and take different nutrients from the soil, so it's important to stagger the crops."

If you don't have time to pick everything you'd like to bring home, the Blythes have an assortment of produce on sale. They also supply bins for picking, and all you'll need is something to haul the goodies home in.

Drive east on Highway 80 to Suison Valley Road in Solano County. Then follow the well-marked signs to German Valley Ranch. During the summer the ranch is open from 8 A.M. until 6 P.M. Otherwise call ahead to find out if you can get in at (707) 864-0635. Approximately 42 miles.

# 9—THE WINE COUNTRY

To the surprise of many out-of-state visitors, Napa Valley is not the only wine-producing region in California. It does have the greatest concentration of vineyards and certainly it is the most beautiful, extending some 35 miles from the San Francisco Bay to the foothills of Mount Saint Helena. Other wine-producing regions in northern California, however, include the Russian River Valley, the Santa Clara Valley, and the San Joaquin Valley.

No two California wineries are alike. There are family-operated vineyards and corporate enterprises; there are small, almost backyard vineyards and others that stretch over thousands of acres; old buildings dating back to the 19th century contrast with modern designs just a few years old.

It is impossible to list here all of the wineries open to the public. For a free booklet that does list them all you can write to the Wine Institute, 717 Market Street, San Francisco, California 94103.

Below are a few of the most memorable winery trips.

Fall is the best time for an excursion to the wine country, because grapes are harvested, crushed, and fermented between mid-September and early November. It's also when the wineries are most crowded, however, so if at all possible do your touring and tasting on weekdays. And be sure to bring along a picnic lunch or dinner.

## 9—A    Above It All

That's how you'll feel during a visit to the Sterling Winery, just one mile south of Calistoga, while an aerial tram takes you up to the white Aegean-style building overlooking the Napa Valley.

Sterling is one of the newest and most impressive wineries in the state. The self-guided tour is especially interesting; you'll learn about the various phases of winemaking and see the actual machinery used along with descriptive art and explanations. When you're through touring, samples of the wine are available in the lounge or, better still, out on the patio where you'll have panoramic views of the surrounding vineyards and nearby Mount Helena.

The ideal time to visit Sterling is late in the afternoon, when the crowds have thinned and the sky is magnificent. The $2 charge for the tram ride can be credited toward the purchase of certain bottles of wine.

Open daily from 10:30 A.M. to 4:30 P.M. between May 1 and October 31. Closed Mondays and Tuesdays the rest of the year.

Drive east and north on Highway 30 to 37 to 29, past Saint Helena and the Boethe Napa Valley State Park. Look for Dunaweal Lane, then follow signs to the Sterling visitor parking area. Approximately 70 miles—the last 10 quite idyllic.

## 9—B    Largest Stone Winery in the World

The Christian Brothers Winery, located off Highway 29 in the Napa Valley, features a massive 19th-century castle. One almost expects fairy-tale characters to come to life within.

Inside, instead of Grimm Brothers characters, you'll see Christian Brothers. As you enter the vestibule through a Roman arch, the small sample room is on one side and an ornate old office on the other. While you enjoy the tasting, take a look at the solid mahogany bar—it's a real beauty.

Huge oak casks that hold up to 2000 gallons of wine and 5000-gallon capacity redwood tanks fill the cellar.

During your 35-minute tour you'll see these and learn how champagne is processed on the third floor. Don't leave the winery without getting a glimpse of Brother Timothy's famous corkscrew collection, which contains over 1400 items spanning three centuries and 30 different countries.

Drive east and north via Highway 80 to 37 to 29; it's just north of Saint Helena and you can't miss it. Open daily 10:30 to 4:30. Approximately 60 miles.

## 9—C    Stone Wine Cellars

The original stone winery buildings still stand at the Buena Vista Winery, the oldest winery in the state. Although wineries no longer dominate Sonoma County, wine-growing north of San Francisco began in this area.

A Hungarian count named Agoston Haraszathy founded the Buena Vista Winery in 1857. He was the first commercial importer of European grapes and brought over 100,000 cuttings of 300 varieties. The original stone buildings he designed have been restored, and today the vineyards are a state historical landmark.

Buena Vista in English means beautiful view, and that it is. Self-guided tours here conclude with tastings in a tunnel carved into a sandstone hill.

The winery is open daily from 10 to 5, and the tours are free. Take U.S. 101 to 37 east to 121 north. The winery is at the end of Old Winery Road, 1 mile east of Sonoma. Approximately 44 miles.

## 9—D    All in the Family

The Fortinos are one of seven families in the Southern Santa Clara Valley who own and operate wineries. Ernie Fortino, a third-generation Italian winemaker and vineyardist, purchased the old Cassa Brothers Winery on Hecker Pass Highway in 1970. Today he and his family work the vineyards, bottle the wines, give tours with tremendous enthusiasm, and offer tastings in a spacious new tasting room.

The Fortinos even welcome visitors to picnic on their property after taking a tour. Needless to say, they'll have a wine to recommend for whatever you've brought for lunch.

Free tours and tastings from 9 A.M. until 6 P.M. daily. South and west via U.S. 101 to Hecker Pass Highway (152), just 4 miles west of Gilroy. Approximately 65 miles.

## 9–E   Candles and Wine

Beeswax candles hang near the fine wines in the cellars of the old Freemark Abbey winery building. This winery makes candles along with its wines.

In addition to a short winery tour, weekday visitors can watch the candlemakers at work in the Hurd Beeswax Candle Factory. This is the place to see bees in beehives filling their honeycombs. Everyone will see the finished products; candles of all colors, shapes, and sizes fill two rooms.

Then, if you've forgotten to bring along fixings for a picnic, the gourmet shop on the property will probably have whatever you need.

Open 11 A.M. to 4:30 P.M. daily for retail sales. Tours Monday through Friday at 11 A.M. and 2 P.M., Saturday and Sunday at 1:30 P.M. and 3 P.M.

East and north via Highway 80 to 37 to 29, two miles north of Saint Helena. Approximately 62 miles.

# 10—ARTS, CRAFTS, AND MUSIC

You don't need a concert hall to hear rock music or jazz. You don't have to go to the San Francisco Opera House to see "La Traviata." And you'll find good art in places other than metropolitan museums and major art galleries.

Music festivals and art fairs are held almost all summer long in Northern California; you just have to know where to look. A few of the best ones are listed below.

## 10–A   The Best Things in Life Are Free

That may not be entirely true. But a Sunday summer afternoon at Sigmund Stern Grove is certainly a rare treat, and it's free.

Ever since 1938 this magnificent lush green park in San Francisco has been the site of the Midsummer Music Festival. The performances, on Sunday afternoons from early June to mid-August, range from cultural dances to jazz, opera to Broadway shows.

The performers are among the most famous in their fields. In other places they command top dollar, but at Stern Grove they play for free. The Preservation Hall Jazz Band from New Orleans and the late Arthur Fiedler are just a few of the visitors who have recently been on stage at Stern Grove.

Obviously these names attract large crowds, even with a minimum of publicity, so it's a good idea to arrive at the park early to insure a space on the grass. A lot of people bring the Sunday paper; a bottle of wine and picnic fare will also add to the day's enjoyment.

Even though the park is always packed, the atmosphere is friendly. Everyone is there to have a good time and listen to some good music.

If you don't like crowds or can't arrange a trip to the park on a Sunday afternoon, a visit to Stern Grove is worthwhile at other times too. The 10-block long park has giant eucalyptus trees and a lovely small lake. When there are no musical events, it's a very quiet and peaceful place, and it's free.

For the summer schedule, call (415) 626-5500.

Located in the southern part of the city at Sloat Boulevard and 19th Avenue.

## 10—B    For Art's Sake

Art exhibitions at the Villa Montalvo change monthly, so you'll have an excuse to keep coming back to this Mediterranean-style structure and its grounds nestled in the foothills of the Santa Cruz mountains.

Montalvo was a 16th-century Spanish writer who described a wonderful imaginary island called California. This 175-acre estate was converted into a center for creative activities after its owner, the late United States senator and San Francisco Mayor James Phelan, died. Galleries on the main floor exhibit artists' works; concerts and plays are performed in the Carriage House Theater and the outdoor amphitheater. Upstairs, completely furnished apartments are occupied by writers, artists, and musicians.

The view from the windows or, better yet, a stroll through the grounds certainly inspires creativity. Nature trails through gardens, redwood groves, and meadows are open to the public as well as to temporary residents. There are almost 70 species of birds to watch and listen to. The villa is open daily from 1 P.M. except on Mondays. On weekends there is a small admission charge. For further information on the summer musical festivals and theater, or to find out about living at the Villa, call (408) 867-3241.

South via Highway 101 to 280 to 85 south to Saratoga-Los Gatos Road. Follow signs. Approximately 55 miles.

## 10–C     Brown Bagging It

Summer's the time—before the grape harvest begins—for a trip to the wineries that offer music as well as wine.

For more than 20 years the Paul Masson Mountain Winery in Saratoga has sponsored concerts from chamber music to jazz, folk, and blues. The schedule in 1979 included an entire program devoted to Mozart, an evening with Stan Getz and Odetta, and the Naumburg-winning Primavera String Quartet, an all-female ensemble from New York. Write or call the winery at 13150 Saratoga Avenue, Saratoga, California (408) 257-7800 for future schedules. Take Highway 101 south to 280 south to the Saratoga Avenue exit, then go 3 miles southwest.

The San Francisco Opera performs three free "Brown Bag Opera" concerts in the open fields of the Geyser Peak Winery. If you can get a bicycle here, you'll really have fun exploring some of the country roads before or after the 2 P.M. performances. Call (707) 966-8100 for schedules. Highway 101 north to Canyon Road overpass.

Robert Mondavi's vineyards are the site of an annual jazz festival with star attractions like the New Orleans Preservation Hall Jazz Band and Ella Fitzgerald. Schedules and tickets can be obtained from Robert Mondavi, Oakville, California (mail order only).

Other wineries that serve up music with wine include Inglenook and Charles Krug, both in Napa, at (707) 963-7812 and 963-2761.

## 10–D     An Artists' Community

A charming 19th-century-style village on Northern California's coast, Mendocino is home for a variety of artists and craftspeople. Its beautiful setting is certainly inspiring, and you'll probably recognize some local sights in the paintings and photographs you see.

The Mendocino Art Center, established in 1959, exhibits the work of several local artists. Arts and crafts are always on display here, from ceramic vases to macramé wall hangings and intricate jewelry.

The Art Center offers art lessons during the summer months. It's difficult to imagine a more ideal setting for learning the techniques of printmaking, basketry, woodwork, and other arts.

Most of the week-long workshops meet from Monday through Friday between 9:30 A.M. and 12:30 P.M. Classes are kept small and individual expression is emphasized.

The Art Center is right in the heart of town near the old Presbyterian church, the masonic hall, antique shops, a general store and a dozen other small art galleries. You'll want to browse around the back streets of this old mill town. You can feed ducks at the pond on Main Street, enjoy a homemade meal at the Café Beaujolais on Ukiah Street, (707) 937-5614; or head to the beach to search for driftwood.

For a detailed list of classes and fee information, write to the Mendocino Art Center, 45200 Lake Street, P.O. Box 36, Mendocino, California 95460, or call (707) 937-5818.

## 10—E  Betty's Pottery Cabin

Built in 1908, the Watson cabin is the oldest log cabin at Lake Tahoe. That's reason enough to visit, but the real appeal is the large collection of hand-crafted pottery and genuine Navajo rugs inside.

Local artist and potter Betty Layton deserves all the credit for arranging these displays, which change regularly. She takes great pride in both the pieces and the nationally-known potters she chooses to exhibit. You'll find that no two lamps, vases, or bowls are exactly alike.

Betty has owned and operated the Potter's Wheel for three years, but the genuine Indian rugs have been there for over 30. The previous owner dealt directly with the Navajo tribes.

Besides answering all your questions about pottery, Betty can talk for hours about the Lake Tahoe area. She's been a resident there for more than 30 years.

Located at 560 N. Lake Boulevard, Tahoe City, on Highway 28. Open daily in summer 11 A.M. to 5:30 P.M., in winter 12 to 5 except Sundays.

## 10—F  The Streets of San Francisco

You'll find artists, musicians, mimes, jugglers, and even a human juke box showcasing their talents and creations on the sidewalks of San Francisco. Although the crafts, leather goods, photographs, and jewelry for sale here have become increasingly commercial over the years, especially near Ghirardelli Square and the Cannery, unique items can still be found. The things you'll find here aren't available in nearby shops or department stores.

The Justin Herman Plaza, right behind the Hyatt Regency Hotel at First and Market Streets, is less crowded and commercial than other spots. Most of the artists here have had licenses issued by the Art Commission for over 10 years, and they love talking about their work. Getting a permit to do business on the sidewalks is no small feat these days—in fact, it's next to impossible to break into this market. Ask for a business card; most of the artists design their own.

Pier 39 is facing severe financial and political problems. The San Francisco attorney's office filed a suit alleging that the city was not getting its full value on the property due to its having been underassessed. An agreement was reached granting the city increased returns. Also, business has not been as good as anticipated, so there's been a high turnover of tenants on the pier.

The kids love this place. An amusement area, a special high diving act, and shows throughout the day by local jugglers, mimes, and musicians provide enjoyable entertainment, so the whole family can spend a pleasant afternoon here browsing and relaxing.

# 11—INTERESTING ARCHITECTURE

With its modern hotels, colorful Victorians, private estates, governors' masion, and even an underground garden, Northern California is a unique architectural museum. This chapter presents some of the places you can explore. You don't have to know about architecture to enjoy them.

## 11–A  High Anxiety

Standing in the open air walkways of San Francisco's Hyatt Regency can take your breath away, especially if you're on the 17th floor. Perhaps that's why Mel Brooks chose this hotel to film his thriller-comedy *High Anxiety*.

The Hyatt Regency, built in 1973, is one of about 25 hotels in the country whose management wanted to produce a group of architecturally unique buildings. No two are alike.

The Hyatt's lobby is most impressive. A huge eclipse sculpture by Charles Percy rests on a fountain as myriad plants cascade down from the multileveled interior.

A futuristic bubble elevator takes guests to their rooms and visitors to the revolving turret on top for a drink and views of the city. The Equinox room provides a 360-degree panorama of San Francisco.

Located at the south end of Market Street near the Embarcadero.

## 11–B  There's No Place Like (This) Home

Every day hundreds of commuters pass a unique Victorian residence without even knowing of it. Built in 1886, this home, the Haas Lilienthal, on Franklin Street has just recently been opened to guests. You won't be served dinner by your host, but a guide will take you on a detailed 40-minute tour and talk about the place as though he or she lives there.

The same family occupied the house until 1973, and all the furniture you see is authentic, not bought to match the period of the house. The place is magnificent.

Before you get back in your car be sure to take a walk around the block and see a few other beautiful Victorians. (The one at 2004 Gough Street just had its 100th birthday!)

The Haas Lilienthal opens its doors to visitors on Wednesdays from 1 P.M. to 3 P.M. and on weekends from 12:30 to 4:30.

Located at 2007 Franklin Street, San Francisco.

## 11–C    The Kearney Mansion

The Kearney Mansion in Fresno is an elegant example of French Renaissance architecture. M. T. Kearney, a raisin grower, real estate speculator, and philanthropist, had it built in 1901.

Kearney never intended to live in the mansion that bears his name; it was constructed for his supervisor. His next project, which was to have been a chateau just west of the mansion, never got underway because of his sudden fatal heart attack. After seeing the mansion you can begin to imagine what this man had in mind for himself.

The two-story Kearney estate was built with adobe brick and other locally available materials. Finishing touches include intricate Victorian details on all the windows and main entrances. Half of the original furnishings are still inside, including chandeliers, hand-blown tiffany lamps, rings, and old photographs.

Clothes and papers strewn about the bedroom and study make it look even more authentic.

The house was originally surrounded by a rose garden, a man-made lake, and an Egyptian-style maze. Today you'll see rows of olive and eucalyptus trees in a lovely park complete with playgrounds and picnic areas.

The estate is a registered historic site and guided tours are given 2 P.M. to 4:30 P.M. Wednesday through Sunday, except in January and February when it's only open weekends. $1 for adults, 25¢ for children, free under age six.

Take 101 south to 152 to Highway 99, to Shaw Avenue West to Grantland; turn south and travel seven miles to where the road dead ends at Kearney Park. Turn left to mansion. Approximately 184 miles.

## 11–D    Life Underground

The 7-acre underground estate built by Sicilian immigrant Baldsarc Forestiere is the only one of its kind in the world. It took him 40 years to create, since he worked alone using only a hand shovel, pick, and horse-pulled scraper.

Forestiere undertook the project because he found the Fresno summer heat unbearable and his land unsuitable for agriculture. None of his ideas were ever worked out on paper; they existed in his head, so there were no plans drawn of the estate.

After his death in 1946, the network of underground rooms and gardens connected by tunnels was inherited by his nephrew, who later opened them to the public.

In addition to Forestiere's kitchen, library, and bedrooms, visitors can see still-thriving underground fruit trees. One tree grows as many as 7 fruits, including a Sicilian rindfruit called cheedro. The trees' roots often extend into several rooms, and treetops poke through the "ceilings." But man does not live by fruit alone— Forestiere even built an underground pond to keep his daily catch of fish fresh, and he drank wine made from the grapevines in his vineyard chamber.

Open daily 9:30 A.M. to 5 P.M. from June 15 to September 15; 10 A.M. to 2 P.M. weekends and holidays in October and May; closed November through April.

Highway 99 to Shaw Avenue exit, then go east 2 blocks. Approximately 180 miles.

## 11—E    Thirteen Residents in 64 Years

Governor George Pardee was the first in 1903; Ronald Reagan was last to move out in 1967. In between, 11 other state leaders lived in this splendid old Victorian gothic in Sacramento. Today the house is a museum whose 15 rooms reflect the styles and tastes of its past residents. Thirty-minute tours through the Governors' Mansion along with a look at family photographs and personal belongings give the lives and work of these political figures an added dimension.

East on Highway 80 to the 16th Street turnoff in downtown Sacramento. Left onto 16th into town, and you'll see mansion on your left. Approximately 80 miles.

Open 10 to 4:30 P.M. daily except holidays. Adults 50¢, under 17 free.

## 11—F    Mountain Man's Home

John Muir's last 24 years were spent in this 17-room Victorian farmhouse on 9 acres of orchards. When you walk through it, you may get the feeling he's still there. Pens and stationery lie on the desk along with nature books, the closet is filled with clothing, there's a packed suitcase on the bed and a 1911 copy of Tennyson on the office sofa.

You can wander through the house at your own pace or; if you prefer, take a guided tour at 10:30 A.M. or 2:30 P.M. Every hour a short audiovisual presentation about John Muir's life and philosophy is shown.

Walk around the grounds to see the Martinez Adobe, formerly a honeymoon cottage for the Muirs, and the exotic plants they collected.

Open daily, except Thanksgiving and Christmas, 8:30 to 4:30 P.M. Adults 16-61, 50¢, children and seniors, free.

Drive east on Highway 80 to Interstate 4 to Alhambra Avenue; turn left under the overpass. The house is about 100 yards further on the left. Approximately 35 miles.

## 11–G    Wright's Western Wonder

If you're driving north on U.S. 101 and do a double-take as you look to the right, you've discovered one of Frank Lloyd Wright's greatest achievements—the Marin Civic Center.

Just north of San Rafael, this imaginative domed structure on 60 Marin acres holds the county's courthouse, jail, and administrative offices. The Civic Center graces the surrounding hills and greenery without looking out of place; even the blue-tiled roof complements its environment.

It was completed in 1969 after 9 years of construction. After Wright's death, students designed the adjacent Veterans' Memorial Auditorium-Theater, a center for performing arts.

The Civic Center is open to visitors during office hours, from 8 A.M. until 5 P.M. Monday through Friday.

Take U.S. 101 north to the North San Pedro Road exit in San Rafael, then follow signs. Approximately 20 miles.

# 12—LAKES YOU MIGHT LIKE TO VISIT

None of California's more than 5000 lakes are alike; each is unique. The variety of beautiful lakes in Northern California can provide many weekends of picnicking, boating, swimming, or simply relaxing in a beautiful place.

## 12—A    Row, Row, Row on Stow

You don't have to rent a boat to enjoy the beauty and calm of Stow Lake in Golden Gate Park, but it helps. Even though the lake is not in the wilderness, the boat ride adds a real sense of adventure.

In the center of this man-made lake there's a hilly wooded island called Strawberry Hill. You can get there by walking across one of two bridges from the mainland. Then it's a steep but quick climb to the top for the best view in the area. On a clear day it encompasses the rest of the park, the towers of both Bay Bridges, and even the ocean's surf.

Stow Lake is the perfect place to simply relax with friends, feed the geese and ducks, or take a walk on one of the tree-lined trails. From the lake you have several other spots to visit, including the nearby rose garden and Japanese tea gardens.

Boats are available on a first-come, first-serve basis from 9 A.M. until 4 P.M. except Mondays. Rowboats rent for $4.50 an hour; paddleboats are $5.00. There's a 50¢ charge for additional passengers.

## 12—B    A Lake for All Seasons

Lake Tahoe lures vacationers every day of the year. In the summer its beaches are crowded with swimmers, boaters, and anglers. The latter can stay all year round since the deep lake never entirely freezes over. During the winter months skiing, snowshoeing, and hot springs are the main attractions. In between, the pace slows down (as do the prices), and visitors who want to avoid the crowds can come to enjoy the lake, the pine-scented air, and the surrounding Sierra Nevada.

This 22-mile-long "lake of the sky" is the third deepest in North America. It is fed by dozens of streams from snowmelts, so its waters are sparkling clear and reflect the sky and nearby slopes. The lake stays clear largely because of the absence of sediment and algae.

Its many colors range from the emerald green shallow waters to the almost black deep waters in the middle.

Unfortunately, future visitors to the lake may not be greeted by these brilliant colors. According to a Tahoe research group, increased traffic in the area has led to serious pollution problems and a slow but visible deterioration of the lake's water during the past several decades. The boom in building roads and homes has removed vegetation and resulted in erosion that eventually ends up in the lake. The Tahoe Regional Planning Agency and the California Tahoe Regional Planning Agency were established to manage growth at Tahoe and to preserve water and air quality. Critics complain that these groups are not taking stringent enough measures, and other groups like the League to Save Lake Tahoe have formed to further protect the area.

There are more than a score of beaches to choose from, but the best and warmest are almost all on the northeast shore. Sand Harbor, just south of Incline Village, off Highway 28, is ideal for swimming, boating, and picnicking; two miles further along the shore steep rocky slopes lead hikers to less populated beaches. Known to the nude bathers who frequent them by such names as Hidden and Skunk, these beaches are harder to find. Look for other cars parked on the road's shoulder and the beginning of a trail near the roadside. Walk down a quarter mile or so to one of these secluded caves. If at all possible, stay for the spectacular sunset.

Plenty of other beaches, boat rentals, and marinas surround the lake. D. L. Bliss and Emerald Bay are two of the best on the southwest side; to the north, Kings Beach and Tahoe City have several places for dunking. One warning: the water is cold, averaging about 65 degrees in midsummer. But the hot sun and daytime temperatures (up to 80 degrees even in September) can make swimmers even out of those who usually avoid cold waters.

Salmon and several kinds of trout are the most common catches in the lake. Locals and marina staff will lead you to the best fishing areas.

The 71-mile Lake Tahoe shoreline afford drivers sweeping views of brilliantly colored waters, the surrounding granite slopes, mountain peaks, and towering pine and cedar forests. In winter the road is often closed due to snowstorms, or slow due to traffic.

To get to the north shore, drive east and south via Highway 80 to State Highway 267 in Truckee. Take 267 south for 16 miles. Approximately 180 miles.

To get to the south shore, take Highways 80 and 50 east. Approximately 160 miles.

## 12–C    Largest Lake in California

Lake Tahoe may be larger, but it doesn't qualify as the largest lake in the state since a third of it is in Nevada. So, at 19 miles long and 8 miles across at its widest point, Clear Lake is actually the largest California lake.

For 3 million years Clear Lake has been at the foot of Mount Knocti in Lake County. Formed as a result of volcanic activity, the lake was center of the Pomo Indian nation, a home for Russian fur traders, and the site of livestock raising. (History buffs can take a side trip to the Lakeport Museum on Third Street.)

Today the lake is favored by anglers (bass is their main catch), especially in the spring and fall when the crowds are thin. In summer, swimmers love the warm waters and hot temperatures, and speedboats leave their white wakes everywhere.

High up in a forested area on the lake's west side is Clear Lake State Park, a choice spot for picnicking and camping. Other resorts surround the Lake. Clear Lake is popular with San Franciscans, particularly because it is less than 120 miles and a tank of gas away, so you should book reservations in advance if you plan to stay overnight.

East and north via Highway 80 and State 29 through the Napa Valley. Follow signs to Clear Lake. Approximately 90 miles.

## 12–D    This Lake Is in a Park

Lake Anza is one of the best reasons to go to Tilden Park in Berkeley. This man-made lake is close to home, if home happens to be San Francisco, and surrounded by real sand, luscious lawns, and plenty of trees. A three-quarter mile trail borders the lake. After hiking, playing softball, riding the merry-go-round, or visiting animals on the Little Farm, Lake Anza is the best place to end a day at Tilden. A roped-in area for swimming has a raft for sunning and diving. The water is fairly clear with about ten-foot visibility.

Open daily May through September, 11 A.M. until 6 P.M. Adults $1, under 12 pay 25¢. There's a snack bar on the property.

East on Highway 80 and 580 to 24 through the Calducot Tunnel (stay in the far right-hand lane to exit at Fish Ranch Road). Follow Fish Ranch Road until you reach Grizzly Peaks Boulevard, then watch for signs to the park. Approximately 15 miles.

## 12—E    Lakes You Hike to Visit

You'll have to walk to these lakes: you can't drive your car, take a bus or train, or even sail a boat or fly a plane to any of these delightful lakes in the Tahoe basin. You'll have to walk, but you'll be glad you did.

These five small lakes in a beautiful forested setting remain a well-kept secret from most of Tahoe's tourists. It's not unusual to have one all to yourselves when you arrive.

A 2-mile climb—which feels like 4, especially if you're not in shape or used to the high altitudes—takes about 90 minutes. It starts on a rocky, somewhat narrow path that winds up the side of a small mountain. As the trail opens out, you'll find yourself face to face with gigantic granite slopes or looking out toward Wards Peak, where you can see the chairlift for the one run on the mountainside facing you.

The final half-mile of the trail levels off and has shaded areas to cool you down. Even so, you'll probably want to jump right into the first lake you come to. Later, after sunning and swimming, you can take short walks to the surrounding lakes.

It's a good idea to plan an entire day here (and nothing too active for evening). An early morning start will avoid the strongest sun hours, and the Alpine Deli on the way to the trailhead will provide the perfect picnic fare. The return walk is mostly downhill.

To get to the basin, take Highway 89 to the Alpine miles in. You may see cars parked on the side of the road; on your right, one small sign marks the start of the trail.

There is one other way besides walking to reach the five lakes. You can take a guided half-day trip there on horseback. You'll pass the stables on your way to the trail. Call the Alpine Meadows Stable at (916) 586-3905 for exact times and charges.

# 13—EXPLORING THE MINING COUNTRY

There are all kinds of mines to visit in Northern California, from a gold mine burrowing 10 miles into a mountain to an open-pit mine big enough to swallow a town. One good reason to explore the mines is that you learn a lot about the history and development of towns in Northern California. You'll hear mining stories and get a close-up look at what their work and lives were all about.

Most mines are abandoned, and some are too hazardous to venture into. Remember to take it slow and follow your guide.

## 13—A    A Mining Museum

There's plenty of gold to be discovered right here in San Francisco at the Division of Mines and Geology Mineral Museum. You'll be able to see thousands of rocks, minerals, and ore specimens, including separate displays of those in each of California's 57 counties.

There are two mine models in particular that you should see. The first is designed to look like you're peering right through the earth into a mine; the second lets you see a mine through the side of a mountain.

Also on display are birthstone cases, a 5-foot high model of a quartz mill, and geological maps. Eleanor Learned, at the main desk, has worked at the museum for 14 years; she may not have the answers to all your questions, but she'll know where to find them.

The museum is in Room 2022 of the Ferry Building at the end of Market Street. It's open from 8 A.M. until 4:30 on weekdays, and there's no charge.

## 13—B    The Chinese Meat Market

The Mercer Caverns were discovered by a tired and thirsty miner named Walter J. Mercer in 1885. Just outside the town of Murphys, this is a good place to stop if you want a break from the summer heat of the Sierra foothills (the temperature outside can reach over 100 degrees, while the temperature inside the caverns is a cool 55!).

This underground fantasy world looks like a landscape from a science fiction film. Guided tours leave about every 30 minutes. Once inside, you'll see amazing natural crystalline formations with names like "Chinese Meat Market" and "Organ Loft."

Be sure to bring a sweater and good walking shoes. The tours last about half an hour.

Open 9 A.M. to 5 P.M. every day, June through September; 11 A.M. to 4 P.M. weekends and school holidays, October through May. Adults, $2.50; children 5-11 years, $1.25; children under 5, free.

For further information contact Mercer Caverns, P.O. Box 509, Murphys, California 95247, telephone (209) 728-2101.

From California 49 take California 4 east to the Murphys business district turnoff. Follow the signs to the caverns. Approximately 156 miles.

## 13–C    Down, Down into the Earth You Go

Moaning Cavern is the largest public cavern in California. About 6 miles west of Murphys on Parrots Ferry Road, it's a good place to stop on your way to either Columbia State Historic Park or the Calaveras Big Trees.

The cave was first explored by miners in the 1850s who lowered themselves into the cavern by long ropes in search of gold. Before the forty-niners, however,

Indians knew of the cave and named it for the moaning sound they heard from its depths.

Professionally-guided tours leave from the cavern's entrance about every 45 minutes, during which you'll descend about 400 feet into the depths of the caves. This includes a 165-stair descent down an all-steel spiral staircase built in 1922.

The tour is educational and awesome. Bring a sweater and good walking shoes. If you want to take pictures, bring a flash for your camera.

Open 9 A.M. to 6 P.M. weekdays in summer, 10 A.M. to 5 P.M. weekdays in winter, 9 A.M. to 6 P.M. weekends and holidays. Closed Christmas Day.

For further information contact Moaning Cavern, P.O. Box 78, Vallecito, California 95251, telephone (209) 736-2708.

From California 49 take California 4 east to Vallecito. Make a right and follow the signs to Moaning Cavern. Approximately 152 miles.

## 13–D    To California!

On January 24, 1848, on the banks of the south fork of the American River, James W. Marshall discovered gold in the tailrace of John Sutter's sawmill. That discovery set off the California Gold Rush and the influx of thousands of prospectors into this state.

Today you can visit that site in the Marshall Gold Discovery State Park in Coloma. Most of the town is inside the state park, and it's well worth spending an afternoon here.

You walk to the gold discovery and old mill sites by a path just a short distance from the parking lot. Every afternoon at 2:00 you can watch a sawmill demonstration in a reconstructed mill nearby.

The main buildings of Coloma are across the highway, reconstructed to look like they did in the mining days. You'll see a miner's cabin, the old Wah Hop Store and Bank, the "California Stamp" used for pressing gold, and an excellent museum with displays of the mining process and mining town life.

The museum is open 10 A.M. to 5 P.M. Admission for adults 18 and over, 50¢; children under 18, free. The park is open 8 A.M. to sunset. Admission is $1.50 per car for day use. Picnicking and swimming facilities available.

From Interstate 80 take California 49 south (Auburn exit) about 20 miles; or, from California 50, take California 49 north from Placerville about 8 miles. Approximately 136 miles.

## 13—E   Wear a Hard Hat

In the Black Diamond Mines Regional Preserve, you can put on a hard hat and turn on a flashlight as you enter a huge sand-silica mine and learn about mining techniques.

Today, the hills in the East Bay are part of a park just behind the town of Antioch. In the 1850s they contained the largest coal-producing mine in California, and over 4 million tons of coal were mined during some 50 years of activity. Then the sand and silica miners took over.

A one-mile trail through rocky hills and canyon land, along with a park naturalist who tells stories about what life was like in the old mining days, takes visitors back in time. You'll learn about Nortonsville, Stewartsville, and the other towns that once boomed here. None of them remain. If you take the morning tour, you'll hike up to the Rose Hill Cemetery where many of the old Welsh miners were laid to rest.

Most of the old mine shafts have been totally abandoned and sealed off, but one is still open to the public. Inside this chilly sand-silica shaft you'll see some of the pick marks left by the Welsh miners.

Open weekends with a morning tour from 9:30 A.M. until noon, and an afternoon tour from 1:30 until 3 P.M. Free. Call (415) 757-2620 about two weeks in advance for reservations.

East and north via Highway 80 to 580 to 24 to the Somersville Road exit, then head south to the road's end. Approximately 50 miles.

## 13—F     Heart of the Northern Mines

The first hydraulic mine in California was on American Hill, not far from Nevada City, "Heart of the Northern Mines" in the 1850s. This method used hydraulic pressure to wash away a hillside in the hopes of uncovering gold-bearing gravel beds underneath.

Today Nevada City is one of the most beautiful towns in the Motherlode. Nevada City's mountain setting has helped maintain its 19th-century character. Most of the old buildings are still here, though many of them no longer serve their original purposes. The National Hotel, dating back to the 1850s, is one of the oldest continuously operated hotels west of the Rockies. The Nevada Theatre is one of California's oldest theater buildings. The Button Works, "world headquarters for buttons" established in 1896, still

sells an amazing assortment of old and new political buttons. The old post office is now a crafts store. And make sure you pay a visit to the Nevada County Historical Museum in the old firehouse; it's one of the best in this area.

The Nevada County Historical Museum hours are 11 A.M. to 4 P.M. every day, or by special appointment. Telephone (916) 265-9941 or 273-9874. Admission for adults is 50¢; children are free.

Lodging at the National Hotel, 211 Broad Street, Nevada City, California 95959, telephone (916) 265-9368.

From Interstate 80 east, take the California 49 (Auburn) exit north about 28 miles. Approximately 150 miles.

## 13—G     California's First Mercury Mine

Thanks to Constance Perham, the world's only mercury mining museum is here in Northern California. The New Almaden Museum is located just 2 miles from the first mercury mine in the state, and Constance is the owner-curator of the museum.

Liquid mercury is the fourth heaviest metal. As Constance explains in the museum brochure, her fascination with this substance began at the early age of 6 when she tried unsuccessfully to put her hand in it.

Now, more than 65 years later, her fascination inspires the same enthusiasm in visitors to the museum, who learn about the process of mining and producing mercury and its many uses. The displays show what the area was like when it was inhabited by Indians, Mexicans, and American pioneers. Constance and her late husband collected artifacts and created the displays themselves.

The mine outside the museum has been closed down completely until now, but Santa Clara County has purchased it and will open the shafts to the public in a few years. Meanwhile, you'll find out anything you could possibly want to know about mercury mining from Constance.

Tours are given on the hour Mondays, Thursdays, and Fridays between 1 P.M. and 4 P.M., and on Saturdays, Sundays, and holidays from 10 A.M. until noon and 4 P.M. until 5 P.M. The cost is $2 for adults 13-59, 75¢ for children, and $1.75 for senior citizens.

Take U.S. 101 to Capitol Expressway heading west, then south for about 9 miles on Almaden Expressway. Approximately 60 miles.

# 14—NATURE'S WONDERLAND

Earthquake faults and traces of volcanic activity in Northern California may seem a startling contrast to the sights you've seen elsewhere. They are a vivid reminder of California's rich geological history, along with glaciers, geothermal hot springs, and other natural wonders. There are plenty of places here to see some of nature's most remarkable and dramatic achievements.

## 14–A    A Giant Chisel Gouged Out Yosemite Valley

The chisel was a glacier, a great river of ice. You can best observe how it did the job from the heights of Glacier Point, which is also one of the most exciting views you can find.

Entering Yosemite National Park from the south on California 41, take Glacier Point Road to the right (closed in winter beyond Badger Pass). It's an easy 16-mile drive, although the last 2 miles are steep, slow, and curvy.

The great bulk of smooth rock off to the left is the first "dome" you'll see. Sentinel Dome was a gigantic boulder left by the ice sheet. In the heat and cold the rock swelled and shrank—and cracked. Rain seeped into the cracks, there to freeze and expand, forcing an outer shell of rock to break off; then another, and another. This process is called "exfoliation," and it left the smooth contour that is now Sentinel Dome. That green sprouting from cracks in the dome is not a bunch of twigs: you're looking at trees.

Glacier Point is 7,214 feet in elevation, over half a mile above the valley floor as you look almost straight down the sheer cliff edge at your feet. About 3 million years ago this was an ordinary mountain canyon; you could have hiked up the sloping sides. Then came the Ice Age, and the river of ice ground its way down the canyon. Slowly, over millions of years, the great chisel cut its way. About 30,000 years ago, the ice melted away and laid bare the work of the glacier. The gentle slopes of the canyon were gone. Now there was a flat valley walled in by steep cliffs. What had been a V-shape was now a U-contour.

Previously, smaller streams had flowed down the canyon slopes to join the Merced River, the thread of water you see meandering over the valley floor. With no more gentle slopes to flow down, the streams came to the edge of the cliffs and poured over as waterfalls. Off to the right you can see two of them, Nevada Fall and Vernal Fall.

From Glacier Point you can get a pretty good idea of how the ponderous weight of the great ice sheet could grind down the landscape. For miles, the high country that you see over the cliff tops across the valley is a world of bare rock, scraped and planed smooth. Knobs and domes just up here and there. You get an unusual view of mammoth Half Dome, 8,842 feet high.

Head back to California 41 again and down to the valley floor beside the Merced River at about 4,000 feet.

Yosemite Valley is surprisingly small, about 7 miles long and little more than a mile wide. Pick up one of the excellent park maps, and in your own vehicle and/or the park shuttle bus you can make the rounds of the famous landmarks.

***Bridalveil Fall,*** to the right, drops 620 feet in a veil of mist. Falls are best in May and June when the high snowpack is melting. They may dwindle toward the end of the dry season.

*Ribbon Fall.* This ribbon of water on the left falls 1,612 feet, the longest single drop in the valley.

*El Capitan.* Reputed to be the largest single block of granite in the world, and is even greater in volume than the great Rock of Gibraltar. You're looking up nearly two-thirds of a mile to the top.

*Cathedral Spires.* To the right, 6,118 feet high.

*Three Brothers.* On your left, 6,860 feet high.

*Sentinel Fall.* Sentinel Creek rose near Sentinel Dome on your way to Glacier Point, and now reaches the cliff edge here to drop 900 feet.

*Yosemite Falls.* You can drive to an observation point close to the thunder of this great drop. Three smaller falls comprise the big one. The Upper Fall is 1,430 feet, 8 times higher than the Niagara Falls; then the tumbling Cascade; then the Lower Fall, 320 feet. Altogether, a drop of 2,425 feet, nearly half a mile.

*Glacier Point.* Up there about a half mile is where you stood and looked down.

*Happy Isles.* The rapids sparkle beautifully in the sun.

*Vernal Fall.* This is the Merced River, entering the valley to become the placid stream on the valley floor. This drop is 317 feet. Take the Vernal Fall Trail from the Happy Isles Train Center.

*Nevada Fall.* Here the Merced makes another and earlier drop, 594 feet. Reached by the Mist Trail; it's damp.

*Mirror Lake.* On a clear windless day, the cliff's reflection is astounding.

*Half Dome.* You saw Half Dome from Glacier Point at nearly the dome's height. Now it's a mile up to the top.

*Visitor's Center.* A graphic exhibit here helps you understand the geology of the valley.

*Tioga Pass.* Instead of a return to the San Joaquin Valley, you can take Tioga Road up through the sub-Alpine country of the Tuolumne Meadows and over the pass at 9,941 feet to the Eastern Sierra country along

U.S. 395. Be sure to fill the fuel tank before driving up over the pass.

There are ample eating places and lodgings in Yosemite Valley and nearby. For the valley, reservations are available. Write Yosemite Park & Curry Company, Yosemite National Park, California 95389. Campsites are located throughout the park and reservations can be made through Ticketron. Regardless of the accommodations you choose, be sure to reserve in advance. If you can plan your visit before or after July and August it won't be quite as crowded. For road and weather information, call (209) 372-4222. Highway 80 to Highway 580 to 295 to 120. Approximately 195 miles.

## 14—B    The Sun Always Shines

If blue skies are your idea of heaven, Carmel is the place for you. Even when it's foggy or cold in town, chances are the sun is shining a few miles south in Carmel Valley.

Carmel Valley is ideal for hikes, picnics, tennis, golf, and lots of other outdoor activities. Perhaps because most tourists are in nearby Carmel and Monterey all day, the valley has managed to retain the peacefulness and quiet charm that make it so idyllic.

The Carmel Valley Road off State Highway 1 takes you along the river past plentiful fruit and vegetable fields. About 8 miles inland is the Garland Ranch Regional Park, to which you'll be lured by the hills and meadows. In April and May the park is especially beautiful with its fantastic array of wildflowers. The ranger's office will provide hikers with a map of park trails of varying degrees of difficulty.

Carmel Valley has a resident opera company, a polo club, public tennis courts, golf courses, and many shops, restaurants, and galleries. These attractions, along with beautiful weather, make the valley more a vacation spot than a place to explore, though you can do that too. For a complete list of accommodations write the Chamber of Commerce, Box 288, Carmel Valley, California 93921.

Drive south on U.S. 101 to 280 to Route 1. Take the Carmel Valley exit. Approximately 130 miles.

## 14—C    Dwarfs in the Land of Giants

Huge coastal redwoods are not the only trees to thrive in the forests near Mendocino. Tiny trees like the Monterey Cypress, which only reaches heights of up to 3 feet, also grow in several areas along the northern California coast.

Take Highway 1 two miles past Little River to Airport Road, then turn right. Three miles further along you'll reach the Pygmy Forest, where nature has determined that the vegetation shall be healthy but stunted.

As you walk the quarter-mile trail into the forest, look at the impoverished soil, which explains the mystery of the miniature plant life. Practically devoid of nutrients, this soil is some of the most acidic in the world. Due to this and other chemical causes, most of the plant life is dwarfed.

In springtime the rhododendrons, which grow best in the acid soils, stand out with their magnificent blooms. Huckleberries abound in late summer.

Drive north via 101 to Cloverdale, then take Highway 128 to Highway 1. Approximately 138 miles.

## 14—D    Who Needs Yellowstone, Anyway?

The Old Faithful Geyser in Calistoga, one of three in the world that erupts regularly, shoots a 50- to 200-foot shower of 350-degree steam at 50-minute intervals.

Wind intensity determines the height of the eruption and helps form rainbows.

While watching this spectacle, visitors can listen to a tape that explains the beginnings of geothermal steam.

The geyser is on private property, and the grounds are open during good weather from 8 A.M. until sundown. There are picnic tables for you to use while you're waiting for the geyser to erupt.

Adults $1, children 50¢.

East and north via Highway 80 to 37 to 29 to Calistoga. Take 128 17 miles north of Calistoga, then follow signs. Approximately 90 miles.

## 14—E    Once This Was a Volcanic Explosion

Back in the geological ages, when California was popping with erupting volcanoes, ashes and lava heaped up thousands of feet thick in what is now a mountain range near the Salinas Valley. Over the eons, weather and stream erosion wore down this mass into the weird jumble of turrets, tufts, and sharp points of rock that is now the Pinnacles National Monument.

The monument is reached by a drive along California 25 through the pastoral valley of the San Benito River, a country of ranches, red cattle, and twirling windmills between the Diablo and Gabilan Ranges. The Pinnacles road climbs for 5 miles from California 25 with excellent views of the long flutes and points of the monument.

In the Visitors' Center you'll see a big diorama of the monument; a pushbutton tape recorder explains its creation and recommends the best hikes. Bear Gulch, deeper in the monument, is rimmed by red cliffs splashed with green lichens. A trail leads half a mile to the caves; these were formed by great boulders stuck in a narrow crevice so as to roof it over. Some of the caves have to be traversed on hands and knees, and a flashlight is recommended.

Drive south on 101 to highway 146 at Soledad, then follow signs to Monument Road. Or you can take U.S. 101 further south to King City, then go east on the Bitterwater Road to Monument Road. There is a $1 charge per car per day. Approximately 135 miles.

## 14—F    The Miracle of Shasta

The multimillion-year-old Mount Shasta, rising 14,162 feet in solitary splendor, dominates both its surroundings and the attention of visitors. Shasta has been described as magical, mysterious, spiritual, sacred, and awesome; local physicists and metaphysicists claim that it is a central place of power. Many of them are former visitors turned residents who found the call of the mountain irresistible.

The mountain towers 10,000 feet above the surrounding landscape. On a clear day its two cones, Shasta, and on the western flank Shastina, come into full view. When the snow-covered peaks are bathed in sunshine, you'll want to have your camera ready. There are 5 glaciers on the northeastern and eastern slopes. All are above the 10,000-foot level, and snowfields and timberlands are everywhere.

In the warmer months, visitors can do more than look at the majestic mountain and its snowy dazzling pinnacles from afar. Trails on Shasta lead through rare stands of red firs—untouched except for natural causes, ranging in age from days old to 300 years—secluded lakes, open valleys, and meadows.

A short 1½-mile hike takes you from the red fir forests and grape pumice ferns in the Sand Flats area to Horse Camp, the site of the Sierra Club Stone Lodge. Visitors from all over the world have recorded their impressions of the mountain in the log book at the lodge.

The Clear Creek-Mud Creek meadows area is a

choice place for another day's exploration. Here you'll see "glacierettes," a mini-Grand Canyon, and a mysterious 1200-foot formation called "Sphinx Rock."

The Squaw Valley Creek meadows afford hikers a brilliant afternoon of meadows, pools, mountain hemlock, and more red firs.

Ambitious hikers who cannot stand the thought of leaving Shasta without getting to the top of the mountain must make the climb in late July, August, or early September. Otherwise, the conditions will probably be too hazardous. Be sure to get special Forest Service brochures to learn the routes of ascent.

All hikers and campers (McBride Springs and Panther Meadows are the main campgrounds) should register at the Mount Shasta Police Department before starting out. You can pick up brochures and maps from the United States Forest Service on Alma Street.

For 20 years, skiing on Shasta was another way to enjoy the mountain. But in 1979 the Shasta ski area was shut down, at least temporarily, because high winds and avalanches caused severe problems and the resorts lost money. The ski resorts are now attempting to relocate on another part of the mountain. Preservationists are fighting this move because they don't want any of the red firs destroyed. Cross-country skiing is still possible, of course, and the meadows are ideal for this sport.

East on Highway 80 and north on Interstate 5. Approximately 280 miles.

## 14–G    For Goodness' Quakes

Amateur geologists and other curious Californians can spend a fascinating afternoon studying seismic effects in the Los Trancos Open Space Preserve, managed by the Mid-Peninsula Open Space District.

Located right over the infamous San Andreas Fault, this 240-acre preserve affords the opportunity to observe close at hand the effects of rock and ground movement over the past two million years.

Statistics show that the land mass on the western edge of the fault is moving northward at the rate of about an inch per year. A hike on the picturesque half-mile earthquake trail is physically and educationally stimulating.

The preserve, with 5 miles of trails, is open from dawn until dusk. To get to the parking lot where all the trails begin, take U.S. 101 to 280 south. Exit on Page Mill Road, then go west for about 7 miles into the hills until you reach the parking lot with a sign for the preserve. Approximately 44 miles.

# 15—NATURE STROLLS

Northern California has thousands of miles of scenic walking and hiking trails. Most of the state and national parks, for example, are full of self-guided trails and nature walks. Although not all of them can be listed here, of course, those described below are a few of the enjoyable walks or hikes you can take to "get away from it all."

## 15—A    Walk . . . or Run

Even though runners have now discovered the beauty of the Tennessee Valley Trail in the Marin headlands, it's still one of the best places for walkers to enjoy the California countryside.

The 2-mile walk to a sheltered beach (it is a "walk" and not a "hike") starts on a paved trail. Soon you're on a dirt road winding through eucalyptus groves and meadows, passing farms and cows, listening to the wind and the birds.

The beautiful beach at the end of the trail is so peaceful and distant from the noise of the city and traffic that you won't want to leave. (A word of caution: Pay attention to the signs alerting visitors to the high tides and heavy surf.) The walk back is equally pleasant. If at all possible, take this walk during the week when the foot traffic is at a minimum. For the more ambitious—those who prefer hiking to walking—there are several challenging trails originating from the same point.

Take U.S. 101 across the Golden Gate Bridge to the Stinson Beach exit. The road veers to the left a few hundred yards further on; turn left at the sign and follow road until it dead ends. Approximately 10 miles.

## 15—B    California's First State Park

Big Basin has 12,000 acres of forests, meadows, and canyons with giant redwoods taller than the Sierra Nevada sequoias.

Start on the half-mile trail right across from park headquarters. You'll see the 17-foot-across Santa Clara tree, the Chimney tree (so named because it was hollowed out by fire), and dozens of the oldest and biggest trees in the area. Deer and birds will keep you company while you walk through the forest.

This short trail will merely whet your appetite for more of the same. It's also the most traveled route in the park, so if you want solitude, follow the Opal Creek trail as it winds away from the nature trail. Heading north, you'll pass the site of Thomas Maddock's cabin. Maddock's family settled here long before the park was formed in 1902. Continue another mile to Commissioner's Grove, where the towering redwoods were named for the park commissioner.

There are several longer and more rigorous trails for serious hikers, with primitive campgrounds along the way. There's also the unique Skyline-to-the-Sea Trail, a 36-mile trip across Big Basin and Castle Rock State Parks.

Take U.S. 101 to Highway 17 to California 9 to Highway 236, where you'll find the park entrance. Approximately 70 miles.

## 15–C    The Tallest Living Things

Muir Woods National Monument is a 550-acre forest of virgin redwood trees in Marin County, 17 miles north of San Francisco. Named for the conservationist John Muir, it was created in 1908 to protect these trees from lumbering operations.

The coast redwood (*Sequoia sempervirens*) is the tallest tree in the world. It is not to be confused with its close cousin, the giant sequoia (*Sequoia gigantea*), which is the tree with the largest circumference and grows only on the western slopes of the Sierra Nevada.

The redwoods you see in Muir Woods grow only along a foggy narrow coastal strip between the southern tip of Oregon and an area just south of Monterey. They live to a ripe old age primarily because they're relatively resistant to fire. The oldest known age of a redwood tree is 2200 years. Many live to about 1000, although most of the trees you'll see in Muir Woods are much younger—only 400 to 800 years old!

A walk through the redwood forest will make you feel very young and very small. Time seems to have suddenly stopped here. From the entrance gate you walk along a flat, well-marked path either to the second bridge and back (about 25 minutes) or to the third bridge and Cathedral Grove and back (about 45 minutes). This second walk takes you past the tallest tree in the park, over 240 feet. Longer and more difficult trails that require a half-day hike and hiking boots will take you all the way to Stinson Beach, the panoramic highway, or picnic areas. You can also pick up a brochure at the entrance gate for a map and details about the redwood trees.

It's shady and very cool, so don't forget your sweater.

You'll find a cafeteria, gift shop, and visitors' center located just inside the entrance. Just follow the signs.

The park is open from 8 A.M. to sunset every day. Admission is free. Call ahead for Visitors' Center hours; it closes early in winter. For further information telephone (415) 388-2595.

From San Francisco take U.S. 101 north to California 1. Follow the signs to Muir Woods; the road is very windy. Approximately 16 miles.

## 15–D    The Biggest Trees in the World

Giant sequoias *(Sequoia gigantea),* the largest trees in the world, grow only in a 250-mile area on the western slopes of the Sierra Nevada. The Calaveras "big trees" were first "discovered" by California's Forty-niners in the 1850s, though of course the Indians have known about them for thousands of years. Although the most frequently visited groves are located in Yosemite and Sequoia National Parks, Calaveras Big Trees State Park, located in the middle of California's Gold Country, has two large groves of big trees.

The North Grove, the more popular and accessible one, has over 100 giants that you'll see along a self-guided trail (pick up a trail map at the entrance), including "Discovery Tree Stump" and the "Fallen Sentinel Tree." The South Grove, 14 miles from the park entrance, is larger, more remote, and has fewer hikers. The road ends a mile from the grove itself, and you must walk up a trail along Big Trees Creek to reach your first big tree. (Wear hiking boots for the South Grove.)

The park, including camping and picnic sites, is open all year. You can cross-country ski and snowshoe hike in the winter.

Open sunrise to sunset all year for day use. Admission is $1.50 per car, 25¢ for brochures, 75¢ for trail maps. Camping inside the park, also year round. For further information contact Calaveras Big Trees State Park, P.O. Box 120, Arnold, California 95223, telephone (209) 795-2334.

From California 49 take California 4 east. The park is approximately 14 miles past Murphys. Approximately 168 miles.

## 15—E    A Berry Wonderful Walk in the Woods

Thimbleberries, salmonberries, blackberries, huckleberries, and elderberries are all thriving in the Russian Gulch State Park near Mendocino. You can easily eat your way through the woods.

But berries are just one reason for taking these trails in the canyon and along the stream. If you have 3 or 4 hours, you'll cover about 9 miles and see a fantastic array of animal and plant life. Coastal redwoods, Douglas fir, and California laurel fill the canyon. The forest is home for rhododendrons, azaleas, and many kinds of ferns. Stellar jays, quail, and band-tailed pigeons abound; you'll probably also encounter deer, rabbits, and chipmunks.

If you like to have a final destination in mind, head toward the top of Falls Loop Trail. There you'll find a lovely waterfall and perhaps fellow walkers enjoying the scene. In 1811 this wooded waterfront area was the site of a Russian fur trading post.

There are picnic tables if you feel so inclined, and near the creeks are about 30 campsites. Those who spend a night or two don't exactly have to rough it, because there are spotless restrooms nearby, complete with hot showers and laundry tubs. Call for reservations, (707) 937-5804.

North via U.S 101 to Highway 128 to Highway 1; one mile north of Mendocino, follow signs. Approximately 140 miles.

## 15—F    More Than 100 Miles of Trails

At Point Reyes National Park, less than an hour's drive from San Francisco, you can enjoy secluded beaches, forests, dramatic coastline vistas, and miles upon miles of untouched land. Some of the trails originating from the park's Bear Valley Trailhead take you to the sea; other, more strenuous, routes ascend into the high country of Inverness Ridge.

The most traveled route is the 4.4-mile hike on the Bear Valley Trail. A level path leads through meadows, a redwood forest, and a waterfall out to the beach. Take your time in order to hear the birds and other sounds of the forest. Bicyclists are welcome on this and the other coastal trails.

With so many trails to choose from, there's no reason to go off on a path of your own, and you shouldn't. It's too easy to get lost in the wilderness.

The best time for an outing at Point Reyes is in May,

when the wildflowers are in bloom, or in August, September, and October. The summer months are usually foggy and windy. Call the ranger's office before your trip for the weather report, (415) 699-1250.

Since there's so much territory to cover and more than 300 species of birds and 72 kinds of mammals to observe, you might want to extend your stay to two or three days. Campsites are located throughout the area. Reserve a space ahead of time, then register at headquarters when you arrive.

Point Reyes is a great place to horseback ride, and there are rental stables nearby.

Take U.S. 101 over the Golden Gate Bridge to the Sir Francis Drake Boulevard exit. Follow signs to the information center at the Point Reyes station. Approximately 45 miles.

## 15—G    The Colonel Had the Right Idea

In the 1870s Colonel James Armstrong set aside a part of the redwood forest along the Russian River to be preserved forever in its natural state. Today this area is called the Armstrong Redwoods State Reserve.

When you reach the park's headquarters (2½ miles north of Guerneville), a lovely walk awaits you along the Pool Ridge Trail. This 1½-mile loop leads over hillsides and through redwood groves. The largest coast redwoods, the Parson Jones (named for Armstrong's son-in-law) and the Colonel Armstrong, will be fully visible. Both are approximately 1400 years old.

After your walk, you'll find it a pleasant change to drive from the darkness of the forest to bright, wide open Austin Creek. You can park in the Redwood Lake campground and take one of the 16 trails through grassy slopes and meadows. There are three camping sites in Austin Creek, available on a first-come, first-serve basis.

Take U.S. 101 over the Golden Gate to Highway 116 west. Follow signs. Approximately 67 miles.

## 15—H    An Educational Hike

Do you know how glaciers are formed, or the difference between Jeffrey and Sugar pines? Thanks to the United States Forest Service, visitors to Tahoe can learn the answers to these and other questions by taking one or more of the short, self-guided trails near Camp Richardson.

You can explore a mountain meadow and observe trout through a 30-foot glass window on the Rainbow trail; see the site of an old historic resort after crossing through forest and meadow on the Talhac trail; learn how glaciers are formed on the Moraine trail; and get a good idea of how the Indians lived during a walk on the Washoe trail.

The starting point for all of these tours is the Lake Tahoe Visitor Center in South Lake Tahoe, just off Highway 89. You can also join a discovery hike here and pick up a brochure to help you identify the trees, wildflowers, and animals in the Tahoe basin. The Center is open 7 days a week from May 15 until September 30. For more information call (916) 541-0209.

Approximately 160 miles.

# 16—OLD CALIFORNIA AND THE OLD WEST

California's historic sites and towns offer many interesting opportunities to learn about its history. You can visit a restored Indian village or one of the state's 21 missions. You can explore old forts established by the Russians and Spanish, or see the grandiose lifestyle enjoyed by the Spanish and Mexican dons who settled in adobe homes and pueblos with their huge royal land grants.

Of course, the arrival of Americans from the east played an equally important role in California's history. Most came during and after the gold rush of 1849, when the influx of new settlers into California reached a peak.

## 16–A    From Missile Site to Public Park

Discovered just over 100 years ago, Angel Island has a rich and varied history: it's been the site of military camps since 1870, a federal quarantine station was founded there in 1892 to be used until the end of World War II, and an immigration station was built in 1908.

The island was also used for prisoner of war camps, navigational purposes, as a vegetable garden for Alcatraz prisoners and a Nike missile site.

But today, as part of the Golden Gate National Recreation Area, this 640-acre park exists for your enjoyment. You can walk through secluded groves past what remains of some of the older buildings, through wooded hills, or directly out to the beaches. Deer, raccoons, and seabirds may accompany you on some of the hiking trails, along with other hikers. Still, if you prefer to be alone, there are secret spots to be found.

Part of the fun of Angel Island is getting there. You can arrive via ferryboats from Pier 43½ in San Francisco, (415) 546-2815, Main Street in Tiburon, 435-2131, and the Berkeley Yacht Harbor, 546-2815. The boats take you to Ayala Cove on the Island's north side. You can bring along a bicycle (or rent one there) and the makings for a picnic or barbecue. There's even a softball field for the athletically inclined. Ferry service runs daily in the summer, weekends and holidays during the rest of the year.

## 16—B          No One's Left to Try Escaping

Today Alcatraz Island is open to the public as part of the Golden Gate National Recreation Area. You'll find out about the history of this famous former prison when you take the excellent 1½-hour ranger-guided tour.

After you've arrived on the island by ferry, you'll walk through the grounds and into the jail. You'll see the tiny cells occupied by some of the country's most notorious criminals, including Machine Gun Kelly and Al Capone, between 1933 and 1964. "Hell holes" were the dark metal boxes reserved for punishing the vicious prisoners who broke the rules once too often. Solitary confinement in these boxes could last for weeks.

As you go through the mess hall and recreation yard, you'll hear stories of life in the penitentiary. The criminals weren't the only ones who were tough; the guards could be equally brutal. The strict rules allowed only one hour of talking per week, very little recreation time outside, etc. You'll begin to understand why some of the criminals attempted to escape by swimming ashore, even though the rough, cold waters meant almost certain death. Only two men ever escaped the prison. In 1962 they tunnelled themselves out with spoons and were never seen again. To this day it is unknown whether they drowned or successfully made their way to freedom.

Alcatraz was finally abandoned in 1967. The cost per prisoner far exceeded that of other prisons, and there were no rehabilitational facilities. During the 1970s, numerous proposals for the island were filed— suggestions ranged from a convention center to an amusement park—but until a decision is reached the former prison will remain open to the public.

Ferries leave for Alcatraz from Pier 43 daily every 45 minutes, but you'll need to reserve a space a few weeks in advance for a weekend trip. The 2-hour tour includes a lot of walking. The cost is $2 for adults and $1 for children. The summer schedule for the ferries is 9 A.M. to 5:15; in the winter they run 9 to 3. For reservations call (415) 546-2805.

## 16—C　The Russians Were Here, The Russians Were Here

In the 19th century, Fort Ross was the United States outpost for Russian fur traders. Today it is a state historic park.

Even though the buildings are fire-scarred, visitors can still get an idea of life under Russian domination. The restored old chapel, commander's house, and eight-sided blockade, which you can climb to overlook the inlet, re-create this past era.

The Commander's House contains tools and equipment used during the Russian occupancy. From the Call Ranch, where the owners of Fort Ross lived in the late 19th century, you can get a spectacular view of the rocky beaches below.

Open daily 9 A.M. to 6 P.M. in summer, and 9 to 5 all other times of year. Admission is free.

Go north along the coast from U.S. 101 over the Golden Gate Bridge to California 1. Approximately 70 miles.

## 16—D　Vallejo Comes Back to Life

No California history lesson is complete without mention of Marianno Vallejo. At age 21 he was already a military hero, having led an expedition in 1829 to defeat a highly determined band of runaway mission Indians who had set up a stronghold in the San Joaquin Valley. Two years later he was named Commander of the San Francisco Presidio. In 1836 he took on a new title: Comandante General of all Mexican military forces in the state. Until California's "Mexican era" ended in 1846, General Vallejo was undoubtedly the "numero uno" hero north of the San Francisco Bay.

Several books have been written about him, but his character comes to life more vividly during a single visit to the "Pueblo of Sonoma" that he established.

Start your visit by stopping at Lachryma Montis, his city house, where he lived with his wife for 35 years. As you open the screen door to take your self-guided tour of this handsome Victorian Gothic home, the sound of the clock ticking makes you feel the General is expecting you. The large Gothic window in the master bedroom and the white marble fireplaces in every room are very impressive. Many of the family's personal belongings have been left untouched.

Other articles and photographs are on display in the estate museum, which was originally used as a warehouse to store wine, fruit, and other produce for the family. A kitchen building, cooks' quarters, and guest house are also on the grounds.

Sonoma Plaza, a half-mile southeast of Lachryma Montis, dates back to 1834 and has several buildings to explore. The Mission San Francisco Solano (at East Spain and First Streets) was the last and furthest north of the 21 Franciscan missions founded in California (it was also the only one established under Mexican rule). Continuing west on Spain Street, you'll come to the Bear Flag National Historical Monument, the Sonoma barracks, which housed the Mexican army troops under Vallejo's command. Next to the barracks is the Toscano Hotel, which was originally a retail store in the 1850s. All that remains today of Casa Grande, Vallejo's first home, is the servants' wing—the rest was destroyed by an 1867 fire. The General's brother Salvadore lived in Swiss House, now a restaurant to the west of Casa Grande.

You're likely to get hungry once you smell the cooking from the restaurants on the square. You can try the Sonoma Cheese Factory or French bakery if Mexican food doesn't appeal to you.

Admission for adults is 50¢ (the ticket lets you into any state park on the same day) and free for children under 18. Open daily 10 to 4:30 in winter and 10 to 5 in summer.

Go north and east via Highways 101, 37, and 121 and follow signs. Approximately 45 miles. Or, after visiting the Petaluma Adobe (16-E), take Adobe Road to 116 east to 12, then follow signs. Approximately 12 miles.

# 16—E    Vallejo's Country House

The 66,000-acre Rancho Petaluma estate was one of several owned by General Vallejo. It is the largest privately owned Mexican estate north of the San Francisco Bay. The Rancho is only a 20-minute drive from the Sonoma Plaza, so you can see it at the same time that you visit Vallejo's city properties.

The original Petaluma Adobe was built over a 10-year period between 1836 and 1846. Adobe bricks and handhewn lumber were used for the ranch; machine-cut nails and other industrial materials were used along with wooden pegs and rawhide.

Many of the original furnishings remain in the family, servant, and guest living quarters. In the old work rooms you'll see looms from the early 19th century that were used to make blankets, carpeting, and clothes for the Indian servants who worked on the ranch (at one time Vallejo had 2000 servants). Another workroom was used for making candles.

The hide and tallow trades at the ranch helped Vallejo amass his fortune. You'll probably see some of the remaining hides stretching outside over the fence.

Except for the "Please, No Running" signs on the steps in front of the living quarters, this country house seems to have changed little.

Cost is 50¢ for adults who don't already have a ticket for the day; under 18, free. Open 10 to 4:30 in winter and 10 to 5 in summer.

Go north and east on U.S. 101 to 116 for 3 miles, then go left on Casa Grande and follow signs. Approximately 37 miles.

# 16—F    Monterey's "Path of History"

An orange line painted on the pavement will take you on a self-guided tour of Monterey's historic buildings, some dating back to the time when this town was California's capital.

The Path of History starts at the First French Consulate on Camino El Estero and Franklin Street. You can write to the Chamber of Commerce, P.O. Box 1770, Monterey, California 93940 for maps and folders. The tour is an hour and a half by car but only 30 minutes longer by foot, so many people park their cars and take the opportunity for a pleasant walk.

In the Stevenson House you'll see the second-floor room where Robert Louis Stevenson lived during the fall of 1879, and the bed from which he wrote articles for local newspapers at $2 each when he was ill. The Custom House is also especially interesting; it was here that Commodore J.D. Sloat raised the American flag on July 7, 1846.

The State Department of Beaches and Parks unearthed the manifest of a sailing ship that came around Cape Horn in the 1830s, and it has consequently been able to find or duplicate many possessions and items of that era. There are kegs of rye whiskey, cognac, brandy, and square nails; sacks of flour, salt, pepper; cones of raw sugar; candles, yellow soap, tin ware, buggy wheels, rolls of leather, blasting powder. The hogsheads on display are big enough to hide a man. Rolling these, four sailors could handle half a ton of cargo.

In these inflated times it's almost unbelievable to learn that Spanish California ranchers got just $1 for the stiff cattle hides they loaded onto the vessels. Sailed around Cape Horn to New England, the hides brought $10 each.

The new Monterey Conference Center on Del Monte Avenue, at the foot of Alvarado, is a modern contrast to the historical buildings. A statue of Captain Don Gasper De Portola of King Carlos III's Spanish army stands in the plaza. He was the first governor of California and founded Monterey on June 3, 1770 with Father Junipero Serra. This statue was donated by H.M. King Juan Carlos I of Spain to the City of Monterey on the 1976 Bicentennial of the United States.

There is a small fee to enter some of the buildings.

You can take a beautifully scenic route to Monterey via California 1 along the coast: take U.S. 101 south to 280 south to California 1. Approximately 115 miles.

## 16—G    San Francisco's Mission

San Francisco's mission, originally called San Francisco de Asis, was sixth in the mission chain founded by Father Junipero Serra. It was established on June 29, 1776, and his statue stands in the courtyard. Two prominent San Francisco figures—the first governor of California under the Mexican government, Louis Antonio Arguello, and pioneer San Franciscan William Leidesdorff—are buried in the garden cemetery and the adjoining church at the Mission Dolores. Many of San Francisco's streets have been named for the political figures and explorers buried here (e.g.,) Noe, Moraga, de Haro). Along with them, in unmarked graves, are thousands of Indians.

Both the patterned ceiling, painted by the Indians,

and the stained glass windows are very beautiful and impressive. One wall displays some of the materials used to build the mission, old church records, and books.

The strong Spanish influence is evident in the surrounding neighborhood. Continuing along Dolores Street you'll also see a row of restored Victorians painted in a wild assortment of colors.

The mission, at 16th and Dolores Streets, is open daily from 10 until 4, with a 25¢ admission charge.

## 16—H     Monument to the "High-Button Shoes Era"

San Juan Bautista Mission, preserved as a State Historical Monument, is a fascinating restoration of the high-button shoes era. The mission is complete with buggies and carriages, figured carpets, towering bedsteads, and the china receptacles that were shoved under beds at night.

The Plaza Square, facing the 1797 mission, is a pleasant place of green lawns, lemon verbena, and flowers. The Plaza Hotel on one side was originally a barracks for Spanish soldiers in 1813 and has an exciting history. Angelo Zanetta, who operated the bar in 1856, reputedly took in as much as $3,000 in 24 hours. The hotel was reputed to be a "refined place," which is something of a commentary on the times since two men died of gunshot wounds received there. General Sherman slept there in one of the elegantly furnished old rooms with 6-foot bedsteads, kerosene lamps, and huge water pitchers. The Plaza Hall, built in 1868, was a favorite dance hall because of its springy floor.

Anyone nostalgic for the horse-and-buggy era can spend hours in the plaza stable. There are all kinds of buggies, ordinary and unusual, such as the Amish buggies still used today. You can see a spring wagon, deluxe phaeton, chuckwagon, tallyho, fringed-top surrey, and buckboard carriage.

San Juan Bautista is 4 miles east of U.S. 101 on California 156. Approximately 100 miles.

## 16—I     The Only Town to Secede from the Union

The only town in the United States ever to call itself a nation was "The Great Republic of Rough and Ready," which seceded from the Union from April to July, 1850, while congressional action on California statehood was still pending.

It is often said here that this move was because the town folk couldn't get any liquor. Whatever the reason, one Colonel E. F. Brundage was elected president. Today, the townspeople set aside each April 7 to July 4 for "independence" celebrations.

The town itself is comprised of no more than a few old houses and businesses, mostly antique stores, along the highway. The unusual town gas station is housed in an 1850s-era brick building. You'll find some great Italian food at Giuseppe's Restaurant. At the Wayside Chapel across the road you can get married or have your baby baptized inside a pink church. You can't miss it; just follow the sounds of the bells.

From California 49, take the East Main Street exit at Grass Valley. Make a left at the first stop sign. Drive right through downtown Grass Valley on Main Street. Main Street turns into California 20 as you head out of town, and Rough and Ready is another 17 miles.

## 16–J    The Largest Grinding Rock in California

Long before the first settlers came to California or the 49ers came to seek their fortunes, the Miwok Indians lived in these hills. A hunting and gathering people, they lived on acorns and other seed plants, as did the majority of California's Indians. One family would consume about 2000 pounds of acorns a year.

Today the Indian Grinding Rocks State Historic Park celebrates the Miwok culture. The park is a restored Miwok village and contains old ceremonial round-houses and barkhouses (used for sleeping quarters), a football field, a new cultural center, and the largest grinding rock in the state with over 1100 mortar holes.

When you enter the park you'll leave your car in the designated lot for the grinding rocks, then walk through the village. Most of the time you won't find many people here, but every fourth weekend in September as many as 4000 people gather here to celebrate American Indian Day.

You can camp and picnic in the park, which is always open. Day use is $1.50 per car; camping is $4 per car per night. Even if you decide not to stay, allow yourself at least an hour here to enjoy the park.

For further information telephone (209) 296-4440.

Take California 88 east to Pine Grove, then take a left onto Pine Grove-Volcano Road and go about 2 miles. The park entrance is on your left.

Or, from California Highway 49, take the Fiddletown-Volcano detour to California 88; at Drytown, take Fiddletown Road east about 3 miles. The road goes right through town. To get to California 88, drive 11 miles past Fiddletown and make a right. Go another 6 miles until you get to Volcano. Take the Volcano-Pine Grove Road to California 88 (about 3 miles).

## 16—K　You Can Pan for Gold

In 1945 the California State Legislature turned an old shanty town called Hildreth's Diggings into a State Historic Park. The original town (so named because Thaddeus and George Hildreth had discovered gold nearby) had been established about 1850 and swelled to a population of 10,000 in ten years. Though it was ruined twice by fire, it was one of the few mining settlements in California that was never completely deserted. Today Columbia State Historic Park is a restored/reconstructed mining town, one of the most interesting and educational places in the Gold Country.

You'll be able to spend at least an hour and a half here. The best way to see the town is through a self-guided walking tour, and you can pick up a brochure at the park headquarters for 25¢ (open 8 A.M. to 5 P.M., weekdays).

Some of the things you'll see are a miner's cabin, a two-story schoolhouse (one of the first public schools in the state), the old Odd Fellows' Hall, an old-fashioned drug store, and a leather shop. At the photography studio you can have your picture taken in 19th-century costume. You can see several old-time wagons at the livery stable and treat yourself to some hand-dipped chocolate at Nelson's Candy Kitchen.

The town still has working barber and blacksmith shops, as well as two lively old-time saloons. You can even try your hand at some gold-panning at the Hidden Treasure Hardrock Gold Mine, the only active gold mine open to the public. Tours cost $3 for adults, $2 for children under 11. Gold-panning costs an extra $2. Open June 15 to September 15 on weekends, weather permitting. Telephone (209) 532-9693 for further information.

You can contact Columbia State Historic Park at Box 151, Columbia, California 95310, telephone (209) 532-4301.

From California 49 take Parrots Ferry Road from Jamestown to Sonora. Go about 3 miles until you see the signs for the park on the right. Admission is free.

## 16—L    A Fort Built to Protect the City

Fort Point, the only brick fortress this side of the Mississippi, was built beneath the southern end of the Golden Gate Bridge to defend the Bay Area from attack. Fortunately this massive fortress has never had to do the job it was designed for.

The fort's architecture is a classic example of Civil War era design (it was built between 1853 and 1861). Walk around through the soldiers' quarters and take a look at the cannons in the courtyard. Tour guides will show you the exhibits in the fort's historical museum, where old weapons, medical supplies, and uniforms are on display.

You can continue your military history lesson by driving through the Presidio. It's hard to believe that this clean, largely wild, lush green area is a military base; it looks more like a wealthy suburb. Spanish explorers established the Presidio in 1778, two years after the city was founded, and it's been a defensive army camp ever since.

The fort is at the south end of the bridge and is always open to explore.

## 16—M    Not Exactly Forest Lawn

The first judge of Santa Cruz, a freed slave, a prostitute, a murderer, and dozens of children are all laid to rest at the Evergreen Cemetery in Santa Cruz. This graveyard dates back to the 1850s. The headstones are surrounded by overgrown vines, crumbling walls, and gnarled trees; it's definitely an eerie place.

But the spooky sights are only one reason for visiting the cemetery. The other is a local historian named Renie Lehman who can tell you the stories behind the names etched on the tombstones. During her restoration of the cemetery, Renie has researched the lives of those who lie within, and she can tell you about the paupers, prisoners, and plain folk whose names you see.

You might want to try your hand at some gravestone and brass rubbings. For this you'll need some butcher or rice paper and a wax crayon. Place the paper on the engraving, then rub gently with the crayon and you'll see the design appear.

Admission is free, but donations to HELP, P.O. Box 246, Santa Cruz, California 95061 are welcomed. Take U.S. 101 to 280 to California 1 to Highway 9 to Coral Street (the cemetery is next to Harvey West Park). Approximately 75 miles.

# 17—ANIMAL LANDS

The San Francisco Zoo is great for a day of entertainment. There are some creatures you won't find there, however, like elephant seals or eucalyptus groves full of butterflies. For that you'll have to travel to the "animal lands" in Northern California, where you can see the large and small creatures that rarely grace the confines of a zoo.

## 17—A    Beauty of the Butterflies

Seeking relief from cold winters in the Rockies and the Sierra, Monarch butterflies move south to the eucalyptus trees all along the California coast. Huge numbers of these orange and black velvet beauties gather every year at Pacific Grove on the Monterey Peninsula.

By fall, tens of thousands of Monarchs have arrived at the 6-acre eucalyptus and pine grove. An annual parade held the second Saturday of October celebrates their arrival. On cold days it's harder to see the butterflies because they huddle close to each other in thick clusters. With binoculars you'll see that this is actually a survival technique: since the butterflies can't fly at temperatures below 55 degrees and can't move at all below 40 degrees, they cling together like this so that each Monarch's wings hang down to cover the butterfly below it.

Severe wind and rainstorms are deadly for the butterflies because they cause them to lose their grip and fall to the ground.

On warm sunny days—the best time to visit the groves—Monarchs go in search of food, part of which comes from the nectar of blooming eucalyptus. The droves of butterflies are truly beautiful; the pattern of their wings is created by a mosaic of powder-covered scales layered like shingles.

Sometime in March, after breeding, the Monarchs return north for the summer.

Go south and east via U.S. 101 to 280 to Route 1 to the Pacific Grove exit. Approximately 110 miles.

## 17—B    Miracle of the Elephant Seals

Although the huge two- and three-ton elephant seals strewn along the beach at the Ano Nuevo State Reserve in San Mateo County do very little to entertain visitors—you're lucky to see them open their eyes or flip sand over themselves—they are fascinating to watch even from 20 feet away.

For most of the year elephant seals live at sea. They come ashore only to give birth, breed, and rest. In December the huge bulls begin to arrive and establish superiority by violent fighting (their scarred hides are evidence of the intense battles). The dominant males then herd and protect the females, who reach the mainland and form "harems" in late December and January. After about 6 days ashore, the females give birth and nurse their pups for the next 24 days. Then they mate again.

By mid-March most of the adult seals have returned to sea, and the weaned pups—already weighing 500 to 600 pounds—are learning to swim. By the end of April most of them have also left the mainland.

The first birth of an elephant seal on the mainland was in 1975. More and more of the seals have been born here as the animals continue to return to this protective cove. Last year there were 86 pups, and that number is expected to increase. The number of visitors has been increasing as well, so make reservations (starting in October) for a trip during the December through March breeding season. Phone (415) 879-0027.

The walk out to the beach to see the seals is about a mile and a half. It's not too strenuous, but it is quite windy. Guided tours from enthusiastic park rangers and U.C. Santa Cruz students cost $1.

Take U.S. 101 to 280 to Route 1, then go west on New Year's Creek Road. Approximately 55 miles.

## 17–C   The Oldest Trout Hatchery

At the Mount Shasta Fish Hatchery, kids will get a real kick out of tempting millions of tiny fingerling trout with a handful of fish pellets. Here they can also observe and learn about several species of trout and salmon.

The hatchery dates back to about 1888 and produces about 200,000 pounds of trout and salmon each year. You'll see seven- to ten-inch rainbow trout along with varieties like fingerling (only two to three inches long), brown, eastern brook, and kamloop.

Visitors are always welcome between 7 A.M. and 3:30 P.M. in summer and 8 A.M. to 4:30 P.M. in winter. From the city of Mount Shasta (see 14-F), cross the Lake Street overpass just beyond Safeway and continue straight until you reach the hatchery grounds. Approximately 280 miles.

In September and October when the fish are spawning, you can visit the Feather River Hatchery at 5 Table Mountain Road in Oroville. Through a large window visitors can see thousands of salmon and steelhead climbing the fish ladder to spawn.

Open daily from 8 A.M. until dark. Call (916) 534-2465.

Drive east on Highway 80. Switch to Highway 70 in Sacramento, past Maryville to Grand Avenue exit. Turn right at Table Mountain Boulevard and follow signs. Approximately 155 miles.

## 17–D   Animals and a View

Juniors especially will love the Josephine D. Randall Junior Museum and Zoo in San Francisco, where they can mingle with the animals, pet a chicken, and talk to the birds. Adults can join in the fun or sit back and enjoy the lovely view from the hilltop here.

There's more at the Randall Museum than live animals, however. Dinosaur bones and eggs will prove equally fascinating to the children as they learn about these prehistoric creatures. Everyone will be interested in watching a seismograph in action and learning about electricity. If you're an electric train buff, you can go downstairs to watch the members of the Golden Gate Model Railroad Club run their model on a track that fills the entire room.

Open Tuesday through Saturday from 10 A.M. until 5:30 P.M., Sunday from noon until 5 P.M.

Take Market Street to Castro and turn right, then go left on 15th Street, where the zoo is located.

## 17—E    Cow Country

Youngsters will delight in seeing the cows being washed, fed, milked (by machine), and corralled at the Bar 20 Dairy Farm in Fresno. The large gray building at the back features a glass wall that allows you to watch the activities and see the cows and their calves cavorting in the field afterwards.

Open daily from noon through 5 P.M., with tours by appointment. Free. Located at 4260 West Madison in Fresno. Approximately 185 miles.

Take 101 south to 152 to Highway 99 to the Belmont offramp west. Turn left at Brawley Street, then turn right on Madison. The farm will be on your right. Approximately 190 miles.

# 18—TASTY TRAVELS

There's no reason to limit your eating enjoyment in Northern California to restaurants and picnics. If you know where and when to go, you can sample a variety of foods being made, from cheeses to chocolates.

You don't need to make advance reservations for touring food plants, but it is wise to call ahead and make sure the plants are operating on the day you intend to visit. Enjoy!

## 18—A    With or Without Almonds

Even if you have no trouble passing up candy bars most of the time, you'll probably find it hard not to yield to temptation as you see and smell vats of chocolate being poured at the Peter Paul Candy Factory in Salinas. 26,000 pounds of chocolate are used here daily. Chocolate lovers will be in heaven as they tour past vats of chocolate being poured and conveyor belts of coconut and rice krispies. You'll see the almonds as they're shaken, dusted, roasted, and chocolate coated; then you can sample two full-sized bars—with or without almonds.

The 30-minute tours are given Tuesdays and Thursdays at 10 A.M. and by appointment. Admission is free. Call (408) 424-0481 for further information.

Go south on 101 to the South Abbott exit in Salinas. Approximately 110 miles.

If you prefer chocolate kisses to almond bars, or if your travels take you to the Stockton area instead of Salinas, you can take a 30-minute tour of the Hershey Foods plant and watch as bars, syrups, and the kisses are made and packaged. You can also visit the processing rooms.

Open Monday through Friday, 8:15 A.M. until 3 P.M. Admission is free. Call (209) 847-0381.

And if you still haven't had enough chocolate, you can watch the chocolate-making machinery while you wait for a sundae at the Ghirardelli Chocolate Manufactory on Ghirardelli Square in San Francisco. Ghirardelli chocolate has been a San Francisco tradition since the turn of the century, and its popularity seems to be ever on the rise. You'll know why when you taste that sundae you've been waiting for.

Ghirardelli is located on the square enclosed by North Point, Polk, Beach, and Larkin Streets. Open daily 11:30 A.M. to 10 P.M., Fridays and Saturdays until midnight, and it's crowded almost all the time.

## 18–B    A Glimpse of Your Future

San Francisco's Golden Gate Fortune Cookie Factory makes most of its cookies at night (one every 4 seconds during peak production hours) but anyone is welcome to watch.

Visitors can watch the special machinery that turns the dough into brown wafers and the cookie maker who inserts the words of wisdom before pressing the two folds of dough together. This could be one of your visits during a day's or half-day's trip to Chinatown.

The Cookie Factory is open Monday through Saturday, 9 A.M. to 8 P.M., and admission is free. Located on Grant Street between Washington and Jackson Streets.

## 18–C    Say "Cheese"

Do you know the difference between Brie and Camembert? You'll find out, and then be able to sample the difference for yourself as you nibble on the four cheeses produced at this factory.

This 700-acre dairy ranch with 32 employees sold

413,000 pounds of *Rouge et Noir* cheeses in 1976. The 15-minute tour past the different stages of cheesemaking, storing, packaging, and labeling is quite informative.

Then you may want to buy some of the cheese you like most and other goodies for a picnic on the property. It's an ideal setting, with hills, meadows, and a nearby pond, a delightful way to spend an afternoon.

Open daily 10 A.M. to 4 P.M. Tours on the half-hour. Free.

North on U.S. 101 to San Marin exit. West to Novato Boulevard, then go 9 miles to Red Hill Road. Look for sign. Approximately 35 miles.

## 18–D    Ice Plus Rock Salt Equals Ice Cream

Uncle Gaylord insists that his is the only ice cream in the United States still made in old-fashioned tub freezers using crushed ice and rock salt.

When you go to the factory and main Old Uncle Gaylord store in San Francisco, you'll be able to watch this process. Uncle Gaylord is also proud of the fact that no chemicals or artificial preservatives are used to make his dessert; it's actually good for you! You can sample some fresh, right off the paddle.

Take a look at the ice cream museum in the back of the shop. It's filled with old hand cranks and other machinery used years ago.

Open daily. Call for an appointment to visit, (415) 648-2166. Admission is free.

Take 101 south to Army Street, then go west to Mission. Turn right and drive 10 blocks. Approximately 5 miles.

## 18–E    Rolling in Oil

At the Lindsay Olive Growers near Fresno, you can learn about the history of olive growing in California and see how the fruit (not a vegetable!) is processed and packaged. After being washed into a barrel of brine for aging, olives are cooked for 7 days in bubbling salt water. When the olives are removed from the bubbling water, they are black and shiny and ready to eat. There's a special tasting room to do just that. You can also nibble on other relishes and pimento-filled ripe green olives.

Tours are given on the hour every day between 9 A.M. and 11 A.M. and 1 P.M. until 4 P.M. Closed May through August.

Lindsay is located at 620 N. Westwood. Take U.S.

101 to 152 east to Highway 99 south to Highway 137 east for 14 miles. Left on Hermosa, then left on Mariposa and follow signs. Approximately 175 miles.

## 18—F    Eggs at the Eggery

If you like visiting farms and delight in eating fresh farm eggs, make a trip to the Eggery Restaurant in Petaluma.

The Eggery is more than just another restaurant; it's also a farm, coffeehouse, and delicatessen in beautiful country surroundings. The eggs you'll eat there come to your table directly from the farm out back, and you can have them prepared the way you like them best.

The Basic Brunch is an omelette (with your choice of up to 6 ingredients), champagne or orange juice, fresh fruit salad, and a hot bagel. This feast costs only $3.95, $2.95 for children. Try finding those prices in the city. Brunch is served from 10:30 A.M. until 2:30 P.M. on weekends. Call (707) 762-7228.

In the deli you can buy fresh farm eggs, chickens, and even rabbits.

The Eggery is just 3 miles west of Petaluma. Go north on U.S. 101 to the Petaluma Boulevard exit, then south through downtown Petaluma. Make a left turn onto Washington Street, which becomes Bodega Avenue, and the restaurant will be on your right. Approximately 40 miles.

## 18—G    Try It, You Won't Like It

Everybody seems to be eating natural foods these days, and dogs are apparently no exception. At the Branstone Bakery in Marin, 500 to 600 pounds of natural dog biscuits are baked daily.

Co-owners Ron Hansen and Rick Marks say theirs is the world's first and only natural dog biscuit factory. The biscuits contain bone meal, wheat bran, ground wheat, dried cottage cheese, brewer's yeast, cod liver oil, and honey. Don't worry about hurting the owners' feelings if you don't want to sample their unique product—they'll understand. But they'll be concerned if your dog doesn't like them.

Rick and Ron run the entire operation, and it's a good idea to call and let them know when you plan to visit at (415) 883-0878.

Take U.S. 101 north to Ignacio Boulevard, then exit to Commercial Boulevard. Turn right, and the bakery is on your left. Approximately 22 miles.

# 19—SCENIC BACK ROADS

If you're tired of billboards, neon lights, and tailgating automobiles; if you're tired of rushing, and just want to spend a lazy few hours moseying along a country road at about 15 miles an hour, then get off the freeway and discover the peace and charm of Northern California's back country roads. You'll see rolling hills, old hotels, fields filled with grapevines, and sheep crossing the street; and you'll feel a long way from the city.

## 19—A    The Road to Sheep Ranch

Sheep Ranch Road winds through 7 miles of cedar pine forest with not a billboard in sight. With the exception of a jeep or two, you'll probably be the only one on the road.

Located off California 4 between Murphys and the Calaveras Big Trees State Park, Sheep Ranch is untouched by modern development and most of the tourist traffic that hits its more famous and accessible Gold Country neighbors. You won't find any historical sign

posts here, though most of the buildings date back to the mining days. There's an old hotel and a general store-post office (closed most of the time). The only new building in town, the volunteer fire department headquarters, looks out of place here.

You might want to spend an hour or so walking around. But you'll be hard-pressed to find anyone to talk to or answer questions. There are more sheep wandering down Main Street than there are people.

From California 49 take California 4 east to Avery. Turn left at Sheep Ranch Road. The road narrows and takes you through a forest for about 7 miles all the way into Sheep Ranch. When the road forks, be sure to go right. From Sheep Ranch to San Andreas on California 49, you'll drive another 16 miles.

## 19—B    A View of Carquinez Strait

The Carquinez Scenic Drive, from Martinez to Crockett, is a quiet road less than an hour from downtown San Francisco. If you're in no hurry to get home, or anywhere else, after visiting Martinez and the John Muir Historic Site, take this pastoral route to wind through several small towns along the south side of the Carquinez Strait.

The road affords excellent views of the Strait and ocean traffic. Drive slowly and watch for sights. If there are several other automobiles on the road, take one of the turnoffs so you don't feel rushed. You'll see the Contra Costa rolling hills and the towns tucked neatly into them.

One detour along the way leads you into Port Costa. Take the Canyon Drive turnoff north to reach this quiet town, which in the late 19th century was one of the world's largest wheat-shipping ports. Several of the wooden buildings from that era are still standing; you'll see them along Main Street. The empty Burlington Hotel and Chinese laundry on Main Street also deserve a quick visit.

See 11-F for directions to John Muir's Home. Approximately 35 miles.

## 19—C    The Road to Two Wine Valleys

The Oakville Trinity Road begins in Sonoma Valley and winds its way to the Napa Valley. This 12-mile route is probably the most scenic road in the wine country.

You can pick it up from State Highway 12 just north of Glen Ellen. You'll wind up and cross the Mayacamas Ridge, then tower above both valleys surrounded by trees. Open your windows and let the crisp country air in. Drive slowly.

After about 8 miles, you'll get your first spectacular view of the Napa Valley vineyards. From this point on, there's another new sight around every bend.

Also in Napa Valley, the Silverado Trail runs parallel to State Highway 29. This road takes you along the foot of the east hills, providing more panoramic views of the wineries. In the old days Silverado Trail was a stagecoach route; now it has been widened to accommodate cars.

## 19—D    Seventeen Scenic Miles

Monterey's famous 17-Mile Drive is well worth the $4 per car it costs to enter this scenic wonderland. From Monterey you can take Lighthouse Avenue to Pacific Grove, then Ocean View Boulevard to the toll gate (there are also three other entrances).

The drive is 17 miles of contrasts: wind-distorted Monterey cypress trees, wild rocky shores, exclusive estates, neatly-trimmed 18-hole golf courses.

You won't see them all, but more than a thousand wealthy estates are in this area. You'll drive through the

Del Monte Forest of the famous Monterey Cypress and see the weird, twisted Witch Tree that fell beside the road, the Ghost Tree, and the Lone Cypress.

Strong sea winds have distorted the branches and foliage of the much-painted Monterey Cypress. The trees are weathered from the beatings they have taken, but they are survivors.

Overlooks along the drive provide fine views of the Monterey Bay, and binoculars will help you spot the sharp snouts of seals and sea lions sticking up from Seal Rocks. You may get a glimpse of sea otters in the kelp beds. And if you hear a knocking, it means dinner is being served. When a sea otter brings up a shellfish, he also brings along a flat stone. Floating on his back with the stone on his stomach, the otter cracks open the shellfish.

The Restless Sea stretch can be fascinating at high tide, when the waves seem to be going in three directions at once.

Of the six spectacular golf courses in the area, Pebble Beach is the best-known. Every January the Bing Crosby Pro-Amateur Golf Tournament is held here.

The Carmel Hill Gate is probably the best endpoint for the drive if you started in Monterey.

On weekdays, especially in March, April, and May,

bicyclists can take the 17-Mile Drive. One place to rent bikes is the Free Wheeling Cyclery in Monterey, at 1888 Webster Street. The shop requires a $20 deposit and charges $6 a day, $4 a half-day, or $2 for one hour and $3 for two hours. Open 9 to 6, 9 to 5 weekends. (408) 373-3855. Pack a picnic lunch, and for safety reasons be sure to sign a release form at one of the entrance gates.

## 19–E    Detour Through the Redwoods

Sometimes, perhaps ironically, a scenic route runs parallel to the freeway. Such is the case up north in the redwood country, where the Avenue of the Giants winds for 30 miles alongside U.S. 101.

The drive starts in Sylvandale, about 6 miles north of Garberville. On this drive, looking out your window isn't enough. In order to see these soaring trees, many of them 300 feet high, you'll have to crane your neck and make several stops along the way.

The redwoods are one of the few tree species to have survived from the time of the dinosaurs. They do not grow naturally in any other part of the country.

Most of the drive runs through the Humboldt Redwoods State Park. Take advantage of the walking and hiking trails, swimming facilities, picnic grounds, and campsites adjoining park headquarters.

Kids love a trip through the redwood trees. The Shrine Drive-Thru Tree in Myers Flat has a 64-foot circumference; the Drive-Thru Tree in Leggett is a 315-foot redwood, tunnelled through in 1934.

Your Avenue of the Giants detour finishes up near Scotia, an old logging town built entirely of redwood. On weekdays you can take a free self-guided hour-long tour of one of the world's largest mills, the Pacific Lumber Company. It's a great way to learn about logging.

In redwood country you'll be able to see summer turn to autumn as rich colors appear in the countryside, and the air turns cool and brisk. Summer rain and fog are to be expected.

Take U.S. 101 north all the way to the Avenue of the Giants turnoff. Approximately 225 miles.

# 20—TRAIN RIDE ADVENTURES

A train ride can be a great adventure, regardless of whether or not you have a specific destination in mind. You may want to enjoy a trip to Southern California, or maybe just a ride through the redwood country for an hour or so. Either way, you can sit back, relax, and enjoy this scenery.

## 20—A    A Train to Truckee

Amtrak has been working on the railroad, and its Zephyr line from Oakland to Truckee is a ride through pioneer history not to be missed.

During the ride you can relax in the comfortable spacious cars and enjoy the brilliant outdoors from your window. You'll pass by the huge sugar and oil refineries near Martinez, a graveyard of World War II ships outside Davis, and orchards in Colfax. And when you finally approach the heavily-timbered Sierra Nevada, you'll really appreciate not having to drive and keep your eyes on the road.

The 8-hour trip takes you through 26 tunnels (12 on the return trip). Traveling by train is not the quickest route, of course, but if you have the time and want to enjoy the fine scenery, you're on the right track.

Schedules and rates for the trip change constantly, so call Amtrak for further information and reservations at (800) 648-3850.

## 20—B    A Seaside Train Ride

The Coast Starlight streamliner ride between the San Francisco Bay Area and Los Angeles is one of the most beautiful in America.

Starting westward from Oakland, the train travels along the level valley of the Salinas River, then runs through the 7 tunnels that Chinese coolies dug by hand through Custa Pass in the 1880s. After the train makes a stop in San Luis Obispo, you'll pass through the little town of Guadalupe where, in season, open freight cars of sugar beets will be lined up on the sidings. They are picked up here for the little Santa Maria Valley Railroad and transported to a big sugar plant just a few miles inland at Betteravia. You'll also be able to see the giant missile silos of Vandenberg Air Force Base.

As the train streaks westward again, you'll pass within sight of the lighthouses of Point Conception and Point Arguello. These cannot be reached by public highway. Before radar and other modern navigation aids, Point Arguello was the dreaded "graveyard of ships." A Navy destroyer squadron slammed into the rocks there one tragic night.

You'll have a good view out to the Channel Islands as the tracks begin to front the sea. In Santa Barbara you can see the famous Moreton Bay fig tree (from the right-hand car windows), which even impressed Khruschev. The giant tree spreads its limbs over a quarter of an acre.

From Santa Barbara the ocean views only get better, and at many of the beaches you'll be able to make out the surfers sliding along the tops of the waves (Rincon Point affords the best view). Out in the water, those things that look like monsters on stilts are offshore oil-drilling rigs.

After a pause at Oxnard, the train heads east through the Simi Valley, then pops through two tunnels under the Santa Susana Pass. Finally the train passes eastward the length of the San Fernando Valley into the Central Valley main line at Burbank.

The one-way fare to Los Angeles is $21.75, half-fare for children under 12. The Starlight carries full dining-car service daily for the 10-hour trip. Telephone 800-648-3850 for information on schedules and reservations. This is an all-reserved train.

## 20–C    Over the River and Through the Woods

You may not be going to grandmother's house, but the 40-mile train ride from Fort Bragg to Willits is an exciting journey.

The "Skunk" and "Super Skunk" trains carry riders across 31 bridges and trestles, nearly one per mile of track. You'll see one picturesque view after another: clusters of coastal redwoods, the Noyo River, ranches, and the orchard country.

Frequently the train stops to deliver groceries to a summer camp on the way or make a mail pickup. It will even stop for just one letter from a young girl to her beau. At Northspur, the halfway point, you can go outside and stretch your legs, and in the summer get a cool refreshment. (If you don't have time for the full trip, you can head back to Fort Bragg from here.)

Nicknamed the "Skunk" for the smell of its original gas engines, the line was first used as a logging railroad in 1885. Today passengers can choose between the self-powered yellow railcars and the "Super Skunk," which is powered by a historic diesel logging locomotive. The Super Skunk, which began service in 1965, has an observation car and carries up to 500 passengers. The Skunk accommodates 63 travelers.

You will need to make reservations in advance for either train. For rates and schedules, write to the California Western Railroad, P.O. Box 907, Fort Bragg, California 95437.

Drive north via U.S. 101 to 128 to Route 1. The depot is 12 miles north of Mendocino.

## 20–D    Short and Steep

For a 5-mile trip through the redwoods and up some of the steepest railroad grades in the western United States, climb aboard a steam-powered passenger train at the Roaring Camp and Big Trees Railroad.

In 1880 this narrow-gauge line ran from Felton to Santa Cruz. Today riders can board the original train for a short but scenic winding trek up Bear Mountain. The sweeping views are best as the tracks pass the Henry Cowell Redwoods State Park (Henry Cowell Park also has several self-guided nature trails and two streams for wading and swimming).

Instead of taking your return trip immediately, you might want to plan for a few hours of picnicking and hiking at Bear Mountain, which is less commercial than the Roaring Camp area. Or, at Roaring Camp, you can visit the old general store and caboose-turned-restaurant. Chuckwagon barbecues are held near the old depot throughout the year. Reservations are required.

Roundtrip railroad fares are $5.50, $3.50 for kids under 16. For additional information, call (408) 335-4484 or write the Roaring Camp and Big Trees Narrow-Gauge Railroad, Felton, Santa Cruz County, California 95018.

Take Highway 101 north to Highway 17 to Felton exit, then west 3 miles to Graham Hill Road and Roaring Camp. Approximately 80 miles.

# 21—FOREIGN PLACES CLOSE TO HOME

Northern California's ethnic towns and neighborhoods, and its special museums, can offer all the fascination of a trip abroad. In some places you'll find that commercial tourist areas coexist with genuine ethnic centers, but there's always something of interest to see. In the tiny Chinese communities, for example, the unique atmosphere alone is worth the visit.

## 21—A    Egypt On a Dollar a Day

Few people ever have the opportunity to go to Egypt. But you don't have to go there to learn about this oldest and largest of all past cultures; you can find a wealth of information here in Northern California. A day in the Rosicrucian Egyptian Museum and Park in San Jose re-creates for visitors what ancient Egypt was like.

Inside this museum, designed like an ancient temple, no detail is missing. The original lipstick cases and cosmetics cases used by noblewomen, Babylonian contract tablets, and tax receipts are all on display.

You'll also see ancient scrolls containing the earliest forms of writing and hieroglyphs on coffins that indicate ancient beliefs about the afterlife.

An entire room here—filled with ornate coffins, mummified nobles, priests, children, animals, and other funeral objects—testifies to the Egyptian belief in immortality. Informative descriptions of the exhibits explain various methods used to preserve bodies, and the changes in the process over the years.

You can spend an eerie but fascinating 10 minutes inside a full-size reproduction of a limestone rock tomb. Nobles and lords were placed in such tombs during the XI and XII dynasties, 4000 years ago.

The tour of the tomb and admission to the museum are free, but donations are encouraged.

Open Tuesday through Friday 9 A.M. to 4:45 P.M.; Saturday, Sunday, and Monday, noon to 4:45 P.M.

South on U.S. 101 to Highway 17 to 82 south, then turn right on Neglee. Approximately 50 miles.

## 21–B    Scandinavia in Five Months

Visitors to Vikingsholm find it unbelievable that this impressive home, a reproduction of an 800 A.D. fortress, was built in only 5 months. Its original owner, Lora Knight, managed that incredible feat by arranging for 200 workers to live at the site on Lake Tahoe's Emerald Bay until her 38-room summer house was completed in 1929.

Perhaps the best example of Scandinavian architecture in the Western hemisphere, Vikingsholm was designed by Lennart Palme, a Swedish architect. He and Mrs. Knight journeyed to Scandinavia and studied hundreds of churches, castles, and private residences before settling on a final design for her home. Mrs. Knight refused to disturb the rugged mountain scenery on the site, so the castle was built alongside the existing trees using natural materials like fir and pine.

A one-mile walk downhill from Inspiration Point on Highway 89 takes you to this magnificent architectural achievement. From the road, Vikingsholm is barely visible. That's how well it blends in with the towering granite cliffs and trees. Between mid-June and Labor Day a park ranger leads a regular tour through several of the rooms and the courtyard, during which you'll also learn more about Mrs. Knight and the history of the house. Most of the furniture you'll see, such as the peasant chair, was purchased on her frequent travels around the world. Some of the items she wanted were too valuable to be sold, so she would hire craftsmen to build exact replicas. The bridal table, for example, had special significance in many ancient tribes. Peasant girls received one to celebrate their weddings, and they later served several functions, from cutting vegetables to washing babies.

For Mrs. Knight, money was no object. The cashmere rug in her library reportedly cost $40,000.

After her death, the home had two other owners before the state bought it. Today Emerald Bay is a registered historical landmark.

You can easily spend an entire afternoon visiting the house, then sunning, picnicking, and swimming on the beach in front of it. Behind Vikingsholm there's a short trail that takes you to Eagle Creek Falls. Or you can hike on a 4-mile trail along the water to Bliss Beach. Better still, swim the quarter of a mile to Fanette Island, where Mrs. Knight had a teahouse built.

Emerald Bay is on the southwest shore of Lake Tahoe, located right off Highway 89. Approximately 170 miles.

## 21—C    Not Even a Chinese Ghost Remains

On your way to Yosemite from the Bay Area via California 120, take some time to stop at Chinese Camp, right at the junction of California Highways 120 and 49.

Chinese Camp was once the headquarters for several California Chinese mining companies. Legend has it that the town was founded about 1849 by a group of Englishmen who employed Chinese as miners. The plaque at the entrance to town tells you that the first Chinese Tong War between the Sam Yap and Yan Woo Tongs was also fought here. (Actually, the plaque is wrong. It was the second Tong War.)

At first, this town looks like nothing more than a few old shacks scattered along a deserted main street. But on closer inspection you'll find some interesting relics. The stone and brick post office, built in 1854, is still operating. The old Saint Francis Xavier Catholic Church, built in 1855, was restored in 1949. On Main Street you can also see the old Odd Fellows Hall and Wells Fargo Building, later the saloon. And on Washington Street you'll find the oldest building in town (now the Turner residence).

You won't find a well-preserved Chinatown here, and not even a Chinese cemetery. The dead were returned to China to be buried among their ancestors, and the living moved on to San Francisco. But a sharp-eyed observer might just be able to find a piece of blue-and-white Chinese pottery imbedded in the street.

Take California 120 east to Highway 49. Chinese Camp is just south of Jamestown. Approximately 130 miles.

## 21—D    China in America

With the exception of the Orient, San Francisco's Chinatown has the largest Chinese community in the world. Take your time to explore its 24 square blocks and get an impression of this exciting neighborhood.

The official entrance and ornate gate leading into Chinatown is at the intersection of Bush and Grant Streets. Your best bet in getting there is not to take the car, but to hop on the California cable car line or take a Muni bus. The area is very congested, as you'll find out, and parking is difficult if not impossible.

Grant Street is the place to begin your walking tour. In the early afternoon, the 8 blocks on Grant (between Bush and Broadway Streets) are crowded with residents going about their daily errands and meeting with friends along the way. Visitors will probably want to do some browsing and buying, too. Despite the fact that this is a somewhat commercial tourist area, there are still some fantastic bargains to be found. Take a look at the kimonos and porcelain tea sets in particular.

While you're walking around the neighborhood, be sure to look around so you don't miss the pagoda-style rooftops and brightly-colored balconies. The Saint Mary's Church on the corner of California and Grant Streets also deserves a quick visit. Its interior was totally gutted during the 1906 fire.

When you get hungry—and it's almost impossible not to with all the delicious aromas making their way to the street from the assorted markets and restaurants—you'll have to make a decision about where to eat. It isn't easy. There are literally hundreds of places to choose from.

On my first visit, assuming that a resident would know best, I asked a Chinese grocer to recommend a good restaurant. He pointed in one direction and said, "Any one of those would be fine." When I asked which one he usually ate at, he pointed in the other direction and said, "Oh, those places aren't for me. I go to Sam Woh's a lot."

I took advantage of this inside information and enjoyed a delicious meal at Sam Woh's that evening, and ever since I've gone only to those eateries that attract more locals than tourists. If you simply must have a few names to choose from, the following is a partial list of restaurants recommended by residents and reviewers: The Golden Dragon Noodle Shop, 833 Washington Street; Joe Jung's, 881 Clay Street; The Far East, 631 Grant Street; Tung Fong, 808 Pacific Avenue; Sam Woh's, 813 Washington.

After dinner you might want to take in a Chinese movie. You won't understand a single word, but the experience alone will make the $1.50 charge a bargain!

Most of the shops and restaurants are open until 11 P.M. or midnight, so you can count on a full day of eating, exploring, and shopping.

## 21—E    Japan in America

San Francisco's Japantown ("J-Town") is a most impressive 5-acre complex. Its Japan Cultural and Trade Center, built with local and Japanese capital, is a reminder of the strong ties today between the city and Japan.

In the middle of Japantown an eternal flame of peace has been burning since its completion in 1968. The 35-foot, 5-tiered peace pagoda is a stirring symbol of our commitment to peace.

The Center is geared primarily toward entertainment today, especially on Sundays. Several parades and celebrations are held annually, including the Spring Cherry Blossom Festival and Aki Matsuri (see the April and September listings in Chapter 23). The exact dates of these and other festivals are posted near Japantown's shopping mall. The mall, a recent addition to Japantown, is filled with shops for browsing and buying. You'll see Japanese wares, pottery, and kimonos.

The West Building is the actual trade center. The showrooms exhibit and sell everything from electronic equipment to art books. Also, be sure to wander into some of the grocery shops for a look at some unusual wares and Japanese delicacies.

The Miyako Hotel, located in the center of Japantown, has some Japanese-style rooms complete with rolled-out down mattresses and sunken tubs. The Japanese Consulate is next to the hotel.

Don't leave without sampling some authentic dishes. The Hisago (1762 Buchanan) has quality foods for modest prices; the Miyako Sukiyaki (Post and Buchanan Streets) is more elegant and expensive; the Waraku (1716 Buchanan) sells take-out orders of sushi; and the

American Fish Market (Sutter and Buchanan Streets) has a tiny sushi counter for snacking.

## 21–F    Another Look at Japan

Any time is fine for sipping green or jasmine tea in the Japanese Tea Gardens just west of the de Young Museum in Golden Gate Park. But the best time is early April, when the cherry trees are in full bloom.

This delightfully landscaped enclave has pleased both residents and tourists since 1894. You'll walk across a moon bridge and through Oriental gateways; a large bronze Buddha and temple make it even more authentic, along with the lovely perfume of the cherry trees.

Open daily from 8 A.M. until dusk.

## 21–G    Visit a Chinese Herbal Shop

Fiddletown, in the heart of the Gold Country, is somewhat off the beaten track, but it's well worth visiting. It was established in 1849 by a party from Missouri who, according to legend, started fiddling whenever it rained and the mines were too wet to work.

But fiddling wasn't the only thing that made this town famous. During the mining days Fiddletown had over five thousand Chinese residents, with a Chinatown second only to San Francisco's. Although the last Chinese resident, Fog Chow Yow, known as "Jimmy Chow," died at the age of 80 in 1968, Fiddletown still has a little of its Chinatown left.

Today you can visit Dr. Yee's Chinese Herbal Shop, which looks pretty much as it did in the mining days (ask at the general store for directions). Built in 1850, the store is one of the last two remaining rammed-earth "adobes" in the state (the 2½-foot-thick walls are made of solid earth). Inside, you can see sections of the store that look exactly as the doctor left it 75 years ago.

Just across the street is the Chinese general store. The store sells everything from groceries to candles and has been in business since the 1850s. The old school you'll see nearby was built in 1852.

Fiddling contests were held here every year on Mother's Day until 1979, when they were stopped because of rambunctious crowds. For the latest update, call the Fiddletown General Store, (209) 245-3671.

# 22—GREAT ESCAPES

A great escape can be anything from a simple afternoon hike along the coast to an entire week's vacation without clocks or telephones. Northern California offers a variety of accessible getaways. These vary in price, location, and character, but all are guaranteed to work magic. Once you've tried it, you'll probably find yourself escaping more often.

## 22—A   The House That John Built

Once upon a time (1887), John Dennen built a farmhouse. Today that farmhouse is the famous Heritage House Inn, set on the spectacular California coastline near Mendocino.

The original farmhouse is now the Inn's reception office, kitchen, and dining room. Lovely lounge areas have been added, and guest cottages have been built unobtrusively into the surrounding landscape. Each cottage has a name: The Schoolhouse (built with lumber from a local school), The Beach House, etc.

As you stroll the grounds, you're likely to be mesmerized by the pounding surf. You can walk for hours along the cliffs just looking out to sea. As the weather and sky change, so do the hues of the waves.

Most guests find there aren't enough hours in a day to enjoy the Heritage House and all the interesting sights and activities this coastal paradise offers. A partial list of things to do includes visiting the town of Mendocino, hiking in one of the nearby state parks, railroading on the Skunk (see 20-C), paddling up Big River in a canoe, driving through the ghost town of Caspar, meandering through the Mendocino Coast Botanical Gardens, and sunning at one of many nearby beaches.

Whatever you choose, you'll return for a delicious evening meal in the Heritage House dining room overlooking the ocean. Everything about the place is first-rate, from the Dennens' hospitality to the service and food at breakfast and dinner.

After staying there once, you're sure to come back. It's no wonder so many people say "Same time, next year" to Mr. Dennen (the original owner's grandson) when they leave. The well-known play was written after a visit to the Inn by Bernard Slade; the title was taken from some guests' parting words. The movie was filmed here a few years later, and the cottage used in the film is now a favorite of guests.

Needless to say, visitors must call months in advance to get reservations. Even so, it may be difficult to get the exact date(s) you want. The price for this escape is higher than at other nearby inns. A cottage for two, for example, will run anywhere from $64 to $92 per day depending upon your accommodations. Breakfast and dinner are included.

If the cost is too high, try one of the other lovely inns or hotels in the area. There are several: Little River Inn, Glendeven, the Mendocino Village Inn. If you're going to be nearby, you're welcome to stop in at the Heritage House for a complete dinner at $10 per person. Just call first for reservations, (707) 937-5885.

Take U.S. 101 to Highway 128 to Route 1. Approximately 137 miles. Closed during December and January.

## 22–B    One Adventure After Another

There's something for everyone at the Point Lobos State Reserve on the south shore of Carmel Bay. You can explore tidepools, take a scenic walk out to a sheltered beach through groves of misshapen cypress trees, skindive, or just sit and watch the surf. Once you've been to Point Lobos you'll return again and again.

The 1200-acre state park has a 6-mile-long coastline. The place is alive with animals, birds, and flowers; more than 250 species of plants and 300 birds have been identified here.

Several trails take you through fields of wildflowers or along the cliffs or through trees. You may find yourselves outnumbered by deer, who stand by unafraid as you wander through their territory.

The reserve gets its name, Lobos, from the colonies of California and Steller sea lions that make their home here.

Roads through the park have been kept to a minimum, and the best areas can be seen only on foot over unobtrusive trails. The views of the surf you get from here are spectacular.

Guided tours are offered twice daily during the summer and on a reduced schedule during the off season. Tidepool walks are held in the early mornings during the summer when weather and the tide table permit. For more information call (408) 624-4909.

Approximately 120 miles.

## 22–C    Escape from the Cold

After enjoying a day of cross-country skiing or hiking at Tahoe, there's nothing like soaking in a hot spring. Even if you've spent the day indoors gambling at the casinos or curled up with a good book, a dip into indoor or outdoor springs does wonders for your body and spirit. The hot mineral springs relax sore muscles and ease tension so effectively you won't want to get out.

You can try any of the hot springs in the Tahoe area, but some are favorites. Grover Hot Springs State Park is certainly one of the most magnificent hot springs settings. There are two swimming pools to choose from. The larger one is kept at 102 degrees, and the smaller one is cooler at 80 degrees. For only $1, this is the cheapest and most scenic dunking spot. It's open from October through May until 8 P.M. on weekdays and until 10 P.M. on Fridays, Saturdays, and Sundays. Call (916) 694-2248. Go east on Highway 80 to 50 east, then south on 89. At Markleeville go west 4 miles.

The River Inn, near Reno, is an entirely different experience. The views aren't as spectacular, but the friendly atmosphere makes up for its less than ideal location near the railroad tracks. The hot springs spa is part of a motel complex that has a bar and casino. For $3 you can bathe in a large indoor or outdoor pool and use a wood-lined steam room. An hour in a private room with a steam room and pool for up to two people also costs $3. $1.50 pays for a whirlpool bath, and an additional $10 gets you a massage.

Open 24 hours a day. Call (702) 747-2722.

Go east on Highway 80. The River Inn is 7 miles west of downtown Reno at 9400 West 4th Street. Approximately 220 miles.

At Calistoga, there's an underground river of hot water beneath the town, so it's no surprise that the main road through Calistoga houses one spa after another.

The emphasis here is more on health and physical therapy than on the simple enjoyment of the hot springs. After two hours of treatments with naturally-heated steam and sulphur water, combined with volcanic ash, mud deposits, and a massage, it's impossible not to feel 100 percent better even if you were perfectly fine to begin with. The elderly have been known to leave their walking canes behind.

Dr. Wilkinson's, a family-run operation since 1952, and Pacheteau's, the original Calistoga resort, are two of the better spots. Prices range from $5 to $30, depending on what kind of service you opt for. Reservations are recommended at both places.

East on Highway 80 to 37 to 29. Approximately 65 miles.

## 22—D    A Great Family Getaway

At the Sea Ranch, you and your family or friends can enjoy as much time as you can afford—$88 to $160 for two nights and three days—along a beautiful stretch of the Sonoma coastline.

The Sea Ranch is a collection of homes built right into the the landscape. The structures were designed to enhance the unique character and beauty of this part of the Northern California coast. There are four different environments to choose from: coastal strand, ocean, meadow, and coniferous forest.

Homes are available to rent, or you can stay at the lodge. There's also a recreation center, and the list of things to do is endless. You can walk or run along the ocean, fly a kite, explore tidepools, watch for whales, identify California poppies and other flowers, watch the surf or the animals that make this environment their home. Deer, rabbits, squirrels, chipmunks, and rac-

coons are just a few of the terrestrial mammals in the region.

You can easily spend an entire day romping through the 150 acres of rolling meadows and open beaches on Sea Ranch property. The Gualala Point County Park is fun to explore, and the Gualala River, known as a "hot spot," makes for good swimming because of its sheltered location.

Sea Ranch also has a children's playground—complete with a fort for wild west games—a 9-hole golf course, swimming pools and saunas, and a restaurant overlooking the ocean.

Houses come with fully-equipped kitchens but without televisions or other distractions. Time here can be needed and cherished quiet time with family and friends.

Call Ralph Kerr at (707) 785-2579 for more specifics, prices, and dates available for rentals.

Drive north on U.S. 101 to 116 to Route 1. Approximately 80 miles.

## 22—E    Take to the Coast

Want to spend an hour or two in rugged country? Looking for thrills and excitement? Want a place to sunbathe, swim, and walk along the ocean? You'll find all of the above at the beaches of Santa Cruz.

The 40 miles of shoreline in Santa Cruz County are sure to provide a place for your coastal escape. Narrow rocky beaches with hidden coves and dunes and wide-open beaches are all within county boundaries.

Heading south from San Francisco on Route 1, you'll reach the county's northernmost coastal area soon after passing the Ano Nuevo State Reserve. This barren undeveloped land looks much the same as the Oregon coast. From the windy bluffs you can watch freighters pass by, and in winter possibly spot a school of migrating whales. Some of the popular beaches in this area are Waddell Creek, Greyhound Rock, and Scott Creek. Shell hunters will have their best luck here after a winter's storm.

Several miles further south on Route 1 is the Natural Bridges State Beach. Here, you'll see two spectacular 35-foot-high arches carved out of rock by thrashing waves. This is probably one of the most photographed areas along the coast. For solitude and spectacular surroundings, Natural Bridges can be enjoyed most during the off season when it teems more with marine life in tidepools than with people. In the winter months Monarch butterflies live, hidden for the most part, in dense clusters in eucalyptus groves (see 17-A).

One mile south of the Natural Bridges Beach you might want to stop at Lighthouse Point to see an active sea lion colony or watch a winter sunset. Lighthouse Point is on West Cliff Drive along with several other stopping points for views of sailboats, surfers, and the Monterey Bay.

Then you'll drop down to the Santa Cruz Pier and Boardwalk where the action is. A giant rollercoaster, carousel, skeeball, and pinball arcade are reminders of the old Coney Island boardwalk. You're only a minute's walk from the ocean. Over the screams of terrorized rollercoaster fans, you'll hear the surf. It's hard to resist a cotton candy or soft ice cream cone.

Continuing south, the crowds and noise fade away, and you'll reach several accessible flat beaches separated by the jagged coastline. To the east you'll see green foothills, mountains, and redwood forests.

Twin Lakes Beach, next to the Yacht Harbor, is great for sunning and swimming. Rio Del Mar Beach is a favorite walking beach.

Beachside parks like New Brighton, Sunset, and Seacliff are great camping getaways, especially in May and September when fog and crowds are at a minimum.

Reservations through Ticketron are recommended. From these campgrounds, you can take side trips to state parks in the nearby Santa Cruz mountains.

## 22–F    Floating Motels

Have you ever considered living and loafing on the water for a few days or a week? For the thousands who houseboat along the Sacramento-San Joaquin Delta every year, it provides a sense of timelessness that is difficult to get on most vacations.

Houseboats come in all shapes and sizes, offering simple or deluxe accommodations, and most of them sleep 6 or more people. You'll have time to swim, fish (ask locals about the best fishing holes), read, cook gourmet meals in a fully-equipped kitchen, navigate, and take side trips to some of the small farming towns above the 2000 miles of waterways.

The delta region extends from Sacramento to a little beyond Tracy and from Pittsburgh to Stockton. For the most part the pace is slow in the farming communities just beyond the levees; you'll probably feel that you're in another era. Some of the levee roads, by the way, make for great bicycle trips.

Watching day turn to night will undoubtedly be a highlight of your stay on the Delta.

Houseboating is available throughout the year. The cost varies according to season, the number of people aboard, and your accommodations. Luxurious cruisers will rent for $50 to $100 per day or $350 to $500 for a week. For a complete list of the harbors and marinas renting houseboats write to Delta Chambers, 1105 N. Eldorado Street, Stockton, California 95202, or call (209) 466-7066.

Be sure to bring a sweater or jacket; nights on the Delta tend to be cool. It's also a good idea to carry a few days' food supply on board, and you'll most likely need to bring your own sleeping bag or bedding and linens.

Drive east on Highway 80 to 580 to 205 to 5 toward Stockton. Approximately 90 minutes driving time from San Francisco. Get specific directions from the harbor or marina you'll be renting from.

## 23—Something Doing All the Time (Northern California's Most Colorful Events)

Northern California communities traditionally celebrate their particular attractions or sources of local pride. Celebrations center around beaches, clams, crops, local history, even racing turtles and jumping frogs. The result is a multitude of colorful events spread over the year.

These are some that appeal most to visitors. Most have taken place for years and, according to sponsors, will continue barring the unforeseeable. Write first or check ahead of time to find out the exact dates and other pertinent information you may need. Then you'll be able to plan your visit to include other things, such as those mentioned throughout the book, on your trip.

### January

*Chinese New Year.* This 9-day celebration takes place in San Francisco's Chinatown in either late January or early February. The dragon parade, with a block-long dragon, is nothing short of spectacular. Thousands of spectators attend the Saturday night parade, so get there early. The street scene is lively for the 9 days; festivities include beauty contests, elaborate floats, music, and of course thousands of firecrackers. For more information write or call the San Francisco Convention and Visitors' Bureau, Hallidie Plaza, San Francisco, California 94102, (415) 626-5500.

*Gold Discovery Day.* This lively celebration and old-fashioned parade have been held for years on the weekend closest to January 24 in honor of John Marshall's finding gold in 1848. The Sunday 1 P.M. parade is good old-fashioned fun, complete with horse-drawn wagons and the Colma fire truck. It starts on Highway 49, a few miles north of Placerville. For more information contact the Visitors' Information Center, 476 Post Street, San Francisco, California 94102.

*Bing Crosby Pro-Amateur Golf Tournament.* You don't have to be a golfer to enjoy this sporting event. For more than 30 years, celebrities from all over the world have competed or stood on the sidelines under rain, snow, or shine. A Crosby Clambake is part of the festivities. Get reservations in advance. Contact the Monterey Peninsula Chamber of Commerce, P.O. Box 489, Monterey, California 93942.

## February

*The Camellia Festival.* Sacramento boasts a 10-day event, starting in late February and continuing into March, to celebrate the blooming camellias. Events include folk dancing, a tennis tournament, a special breakfast, and of course a big camellia show. Write the Camellia Festival Association, 724 J. Street #101, Sacramento, California 95814.

*Citrus Fair and Parade.* Every year this parade marches the same route from the Citrus Pavilion fairgrounds through downtown Cloverdale, 30 miles north of Santa Rosa on U.S. 101. But its theme changes annually. Spectators delight in all the exhibits, from citrus products to arts and crafts. Write the Cloverdale Chamber of Commerce, Citrus Fair Building, Cloverdale, California 95425.

## March

*Kite-Flying Festival.* Kite flyers of all ages launch their homemade and sometimes exotic inventions at the Carmel Middle School athletic field, usually on the first Saturday in March. You don't have to enter the competition to enjoy the festival. Carmel Chamber of Commerce, San Carlos and 7th Avenue, Carmel, California 93921.

*Pinnacles Wildflower Show.* If the weather has been right, a visit to the Pinnacles National Monument in late March or early April is a spectacle to behold. Pinnacles National Monument Headquarters, King City, California 93930.

*Sunset Gardens.* March is the month to tour through the magnificent gardens at the publishing headquarters of Sunset Magazine in Menlo Park. Acres of gardens are filled with flowers and trees native to different parts of the west coast. Sunset Magazine, Willow and Middlefield Roads, between U.S. 101 and El Camino Real. Gardens are open 9 A.M. through 4:30 P.M. (415) 321-3600.

# April

*Opening Day on the San Francisco Bay.* Officially, the first day of the sailing season is the last Sunday in April. From a boat or on shore, it's beautiful to watch the thousands of multi-colored craft in motion on the bay. By 10:30 A.M. the parade of boats is well under way. San Francisco Convention and Visitors' Bureau, Hallidie Plaza, San Francisco, California 94102.

*Apple Blossom Festival.* The 3-day Apple Blossom Festival in Sebastopol includes folk dancing, a barbecue, a horseshow, and a Saturday parade. The main feature, however, is a special drive-yourself tour through blossoming orchards. Sebastopol Chamber of Commerce, 7765 Healdsburg Avenue, Sebastopol, California 95472.

*Rhododendron Festival.* Beginning the last Saturday in April, this 9-day festival in Eureka has everything from sports car races to horsepitching, arts and crafts exhibits, displays of native Indian artifacts, and assorted contests. At the Rhododendron Ball the Queen is crowned. Visitors' Information Center, 476 Post Street, San Francisco, California 94102.

*Old Adobe Tours.* You can visit some of the old adobes in Monterey any time of the year, but others can be toured only during the last weekend of the month. Old Adobe Tours, Box 805, Monterey, California 93940.

*Cherry Blossom Festival.* For 10 days at the end of April, Japan celebrates its cultural heritage in San Francisco's Japantown. The variety of events includes traditional tea ceremonies, special flower shows, music, song, dance, and of course the cherry blossoms. San Francisco Convention and Visitors' Bureau, Hallidie Plaza, San Francisco, California 94102.

*Daffodil Hill Blooms.* In the Mother Lode country, April is the time to see both old and newly-planted daffodils blossoming on the hillside. There's nothing quite like this unique and beautiful sight. Daffodil Hill is 3 miles north of Volcano.

# May

*Fireman's Muster.* All fire engines built by hand before 1895 are eligible to participate in Columbia's annual parade and contest. Sonora Pass Vacationland, Box 607, Columbia, California 95310.

*Silver Dollar Fair.* An open rodeo, horse show, carnival, and livestock exhibition are the highlights of this event, held in Chico for 6 days at the end of the month. Visitors' Information Center, 476 Post Street, San Francisco, California 94102.

*Chamarita Festival.* According to an old legend, the Portuguese community of Pescadero was saved from starvation centuries ago by the Holy Spirit, who sent in a foreign ship loaded with food. In remembrance of this event, a special folk festival and parade are held every year on the sixth Sunday after Easter. After the parade marches to the Catholic Church in the morning, everyone is treated to a free barbecue. You'll hear the town's school bands, and see former queens and the newly-crowned queen in full splendor. Visitors' Information Center, 476 Post Street, San Francisco, California 94102.

*Latin American Fiesta.* In addition to the musicians and dancers performing at this San Francisco spectacular parade, there will be plenty of novelty entries. The fiesta is a 2-day event with a coronation ball. San Francisco Convention and Visitors' Bureau, Hallidie Plaza, San Francisco, California 94102.

*Bay-to-Breakers.* The San Francisco Examiner sponsors this marathon, which has been run for over 60 years. In 1974 approximately 4000 runners raced the Olympic distance course of 26 miles, 385 yards, from Spear and Howard Streets in San Francisco to the Great Highway along the Pacific Ocean. In 1979, 18,000 runners started the race. The Hayes Street Hill is known for eliminating a fair share of contestants each year. The San Francisco Examiner, 110 Fifth Street, San Francisco, California 94103.

*Dixieland Jubilee.* Old Sacramento celebrates in a big way every Memorial Day Weekend from Friday noon until Monday. Bands from all over the world contribute to this wonderful jazz festival. You'll have as many as 25 places to choose from for listening to Dixieland music, and close to 85,000 people to listen with. Jubilee Headquarters, 1011 Second Avenue, Sacramento, California 95814.

*Wildflower Show.* The Oakland Museum houses live plants and flowers during this special show the first weekend in May. Be sure to explore the art, history, and natural science exhibits in this first-class California museum. The Oakland Museum, 1000 Oak Street, Oakland, California 94607.

*Laguna Seca Races.* Sports car races are a big event near the Monterey Peninsula. A wide range of competitors and spectators contribute to the excitement and color of the races. Box 2078, Monterey, California 93940.

*The Mountain Play.* Ever since 1913, the Mountain Play Association has made the Mount Tamalpais natural amphitheater the site of its annual performances. The Association performs a variety of dramatic works in this ideal natural setting. Marin County Chamber of Commerce, 824 Fifth Avenue, San Rafael, California 94901.

*Calaveras County Jumping Frog Jubilee.* During these crazy 4 days in Angels Camp, frogs try to outdistance each other—jumps of over 20 feet have been recorded—and people from all over the world watch the action up close. This contest was inspired by a Mark Twain tale. The fair and exhibits that run throughout the contest provide added entertainment. Calaveras Fairgrounds Office, P.O. Box 96, Angels Camp, California 95222.

*American Indian Pow Wow.* All kinds of Indian songs, dances, foods, arts and crafts, and exhibits highlight the action at the Bret Harte School in Hayward. Chamber of Commerce, 22300 Foothill Boulevard, Hayward, California 95451.

## June

*Antique Show.* The Community Center at 276 E. Napa Street in Sonoma lures antique lovers during this 3-day event. Antiques are on display and for sale. Homemade foods are an added attraction. Sonoma Valley Chamber of Commerce, 461 First Street, Sonoma, California 95476.

*Stanford Summer Festival of the Arts.* At Stanford, summer (from mid-June to mid-August) means music: jazz, opera, symphonies, chamber ensembles. Lectures, exhibitions, and theater and dance groups also perform. Stanford Summer Festivals, P.O. Box 3006, Stanford, California 94305.

*Salmon Festival.*  Salmon never tasted so good! On the last Sunday in June the city of Klamath holds its annual salmon barbecue along with logging contests, Indian dances, games, and lots of local activities. Visitors' Information Center, 476 Post Street, San Francisco, California 94102.

*Stumptown Days.*  On the first weekend in June, Guerneville residents live it up and visitors can enjoy the parade, rodeo, and Saturday night barbecue. This is a lively event! Guerneville Chamber of Commerce, 14034 Armstrong Woods Road, Guerneville, California 95446.

*Secession Day.* In the 19th century one Mother Lode town, Rough and Ready, attempted to secede from the country (protesting taxation and the lack of law and order) to become an independent republic (see 16-I), but their independence was short-lived. Every year, on the last Sunday in June, there's a high-spirited celebration of this town's colorful past. Visitors' Information Center, 476 Post Street, San Francisco, California 94102.

*San Francisco Street Fairs.*  Every weekend throughout the summer, local San Francisco neighborhoods hold street fairs. Street artists, mimes, and musicians travel from one block party to the next. San Francisco Convention and Visitors' Bureau, Hallidie Plaza, San Francisco, California 94102.

*Inverness Music Festival.*  This is one of several concerts and performances held throughout the summer in Marin county. No matter what kind of music you like best, this festival will probably have it. Marin County Chamber of Commerce, 824 Fifth Avenue, San Rafael, California 94901.

*Montalvo Summer Music Festival.*  At the Villa Montalvo, the hills are alive with the sound of music all summer long. The weekend festivals include classical music, opera, quartets, and recitals. Concerts are held in the outdoor amphitheater of Carriage House. Montalvo Center for the Arts, P.O. Box 158, Saratoga, California 95070.

*Livermore Rodeo.* This was one of the first big-time national circuit rodeos. Touring cowboys put on a good show, at least in Livermore. The rodeo usually takes place the first weekend in June. Visitors' Information Center, 476 Post Street, San Francisco, California 94102.

## July

*County Fairs.* County fairs are held by individual counties in Northern California, most often during the month of July. Each one is unique and colorful. For specific information, write the Local Chamber of Commerce.

*Feast of Lanterns.* The highlight of this week-long event in Pacific Grove is on Saturday night, when lighted boats arrive from Monterey and Chinese-costumed men and women re-create legendary tales. For more than 35 years there has been a parade of lighted lanterns through the town. During the week there is a children's pet parade. Pacific Grove Chamber of Commerce, P.O. Box 167, Pacific Grove, California 93950.

*Scottish Highland Games.* Hundreds of Scots in bright tartans participate in the Highland Games held at Collins Field in Pebble Beach on the third Sunday in July. The games include bagpipe bands, highland dancing contests, and traditional games like throwing hammers and putting stones. Monterey Peninsula Chamber of Commerce, P.O. Box 489, Monterey, California 93942.

*California Rodeo.* Wild horse races are the highlight of the state's biggest rodeo held in Salinas the third week of July. Thousands of horses march in the parade, and cowboys take to the arena to ride broncos, wrestle steers, and rope calves. Visitors' Information Center, 476 Post Street, San Francisco, California 94102.

*Tanabata Star Festival.* Of all the Japanese festivals held in San Francisco's Japantown, this "love festival" is, of course, the most romantic. Held the weekend after July 4th, all the exhibitions and demonstrations are colorful, and free. San Francisco Convention and Visitors' Bureau, Hallidie Plaza, San Francisco, California 94102.

*Frontier Days.* In Willits, three days (July 3-5) are crammed with livestock shows, a rodeo, carnivals, and arts and crafts exhibits. Visitors' Information Center, 476 Post Street, San Francisco, California 94102.

## August

*California State Fair.* California's biggest state fair is a 10-day event held in Sacramento, and visitors will certainly need more than a day to see all the action: livestock auctions, arts and crafts exhibits, open rodeo. Crowds are everywhere! California State Chamber of Commerce, 415 Capitol Mall, Sacramento, California 95814.

*Statewide Art Show.* For 3 days at the end of August, Santa Rosa's Veteran's Memorial Building is transformed into a museum where visitors can browse and/or buy. The show is held at 1351 Maple Avenue (just north of Highway 12). For more information contact El Meyer at (707) 887-2555.

*Paul Bunyan Days.* This mythical folk hero will never be forgotten, at least not in Fort Bragg. Every year 4 days are set aside for dancing, carnivals, contests, and a parade. Chamber of Commerce, Fort Bragg, California 95437.

*Renaissance Pleasure Faire.* This re-creation of Elizabethan times is complete with jugglers, fire eaters, puppet shows, and hand-crafted wares. Colorful costumes add to the flavor of this event at Oak Forest in Marin. Pitch-the-hay is one of several games, and pork pasties are one of the traditional English foods. Renaissance Faire, #18104, San Francisco, California 94118.

*Concours d'Elégance.* Several cities and towns hold automobile shows during the year, but the one in Pebble Beach at the Del Monte Lodge is one of the best and oldest. It may not be held much longer, so be sure to contact the Monterey Peninsula Chamber of Commerce, P.O. Box 489, Monterey, California 93942.

*Old Adobe Days Fiesta.* The life of the Adobe Indians is celebrated in mid-August at the Petaluma Adobe or Old Adobe State Park. Festivities include a milking contest, horseshoe tournament, and parade. Petaluma Area Chamber of Commerce, 314 Western Avenue, Petaluma California 94952.

## September

*Walnut Festival.* Where else but Walnut Creek for a 4-day festival in honor of the walnut? Highlights include a songfest, fashion show, folk dancing, and a marathon race. Visitors' Information Center, 476 Post Street, San Francisco, California 94102.

*Scottish Gathering and Games.* For more than 100 years the clans have gathered together for a rendering of the most traditional Highland Games. This event is held at the Santa Rosa Fairgrounds on the weekend before Labor Day, and visitors can learn everything they want to know about Scottish Highland Games. Santa Rosa Chamber of Commerce, 637 First Street, Santa Rosa, California 95404.

*Valley of the Moon Vintage Festival.* The Sonoma Plaza comes to life with an old-time celebration that includes wine tastings, folk dancing, and auctions. The colorful history of this area, once under General Vallejo's command, is very much alive in the present. Sonoma Chamber of Commerce, 461 First Street, Sonoma, California 95476.

*Aki Matsuri.* Included in Japantown's 2-day fall festival are demonstrations of the martial arts and cooking. Traditional tea ceremonies, songs, and a bonsai show are other features of this celebration.

*Begonia Festival.* In Capitola, children of all ages create sand fantasies during the annual sand sculpture contest. Flower-covered boats cruise down Soquel Creek and an arts and crafts fair delights visitors. All this and more at the annual Capitola Begonia Festival, P.O. Box 501, Capitola, California 95010.

*Monterey Jazz Festival.* This festival is the oldest and one of the best continuous jazz musicals in the United States. Five full-length concerts are usually packed into 3 days. For more than 30 years jazz musicians like Dizzy Gillespie, Duke Ellington, and Count Basie have been performing at the Monterey County Fairgrounds. Jazz Festival, Box JAZZ, Monterey, California 95940.

*Municipal Outdoor Art Festival.* Arts and crafts are displayed and sold for 5 days near the end of September in San Francisco's Civic Center Plaza. The works of many of these artists are later purchased to be displayed in public buildings. San Francisco Convention and

Visitors' Bureau, Hallidie Plaza, San Francisco, California 94102.

**San Quentin Art Show and Sale.** This display and sale are held at the gates of the San Quentin Prison. You can purchase jewelry, leatherwork, sculptures, and paintings. Chamber of Commerce, 455 Capitol Mall, Sacramento, California 95814.

## October

**International Film Festival.** For 12 days in October, films from all over the world are shown at the Palace of Fine Arts Theater and the Castro. Special speakers and events are added attractions. Film Festival, 1409 Bush Street, San Francisco, California 94109.

**Butterfly Parade.** On the second Saturday of October a butterfly parade is held in Pacific Grove to celebrate the arrival of thousands of big orange and black Monarch butterflies. If it's a sunny day, you'll see the butterflies as well as the parade. Otherwise they'll be hidden in the eucalyptus groves. Chamber of Commerce, P.O. Box 167, Pacific Grove, California 93950.

**Laguna Seca Races.** A 3-day road-racing meet takes place in October at the Laguna Seca Raceway. The Can-Am is a regional spectator event. Box 2078, Monterey, California 93940.

**Grape Festival.** For more than 80 years the first Saturday in October has been reserved for a celebration of the grape harvest. Special children's games are set up in the Marin Veterans' Memorial Building while the adults indulge in wine tasting. Grapes and other foods are for sale. Marin County Chamber of Commerce, 824 Fifth Avenue, San Rafael, California 94901.

## November

**Thanksgiving Festival.** The Thanksgiving Festival is one of the liveliest times of the year at the Mendocino Art Center. You can purchase anything from macramé to woodwork. Many of the local artists attend this 2-day festival. Mendocino Art Center, P.O. Box 36, Mendocino, California 95460.

**Children's Christmas Balloon Parade.** Children of all ages parade in downtown Sacramento on the Saturday after Thanksgiving during this lively and colorful event. California State Chamber of Commerce, 414 Capitol Mall, Sacramento, California 95814.

# December

*Christmas Tree Ceremony.* You can visit the General Grant Tree in the Grant Grove of Kings Canyon National Park any time of the year. But on the Sunday afternoon before Christmas, you can participate in a special ceremony as a wreath is placed on the tree and Christmas carols are sung. In the past the tree was decorated with Christmas lights, but the energy shortage ended that part of the celebration. Chamber of Commerce, 2331 Fresno Street, Fresno, California 93721.

*Our Lady of Guadalupe.* Around December 12 the Mission San Juan Bautista, parishioners honor the patroness of the Mexican people with a predawn candlelight procession and service. The day also includes Mexican music, games, and food. Chamber of Commerce, 319 Third Street, San Juan Bautista, California 95045.

*Yuletide Show.* During the first weekend of December, handmade arts and crafts are on display and for sale at the Villa Montalvo. Montalvo Cener for the Arts, P.O. Box 158, Saratoga, California 95070.

*Christmas Parades.* All over California, marching bands, elaborate floats, vessels decorated with lights, and festive citizens celebrate Christmas with a parade in their hometown or city. Visitors' Information Center, 476 Post Street, San Francisco, California 94102.

# 24—FAMOUS TRAVELS

Where do California's most prominent citizens like to vacation? Where do they go to get away from it all, and how do they get there? We asked well-known athletes, musicians, business people, newscasters, reporters, and politicians what their favorite vacations are. Below is a sampling of responses.

*Robert Lurie, owner of the San Francisco Giants:* "I can think of no better way to spend a weekend, especially with the family, than to come to the ballpark. Candlestick [Ballpark] is nearby, inexpensive fun well-serviced by public transportation. That really helps during the gas shortage.

"I spend every weekend at Candlestick from April until October—except, of course, when the team is on the road. It's a great adventure."

*Reg Murphy, publisher/editor of the San Francisco Examiner:* "If there is a happier weekend than to drive from San Francisco to Mendocino and stay at the Heritage House, I have not had the pleasure. To drive up through the Napa Valley and on through the stately redwoods is a good way to begin, and my heart soars on Sunday afternoon driving back down the coastal cliffs."

*W. R. Hearst, Jr., Editor-in-Chief, Hearst Newspapers:* ". . . the most scenic trip is the run from San Simeon up to Monterey. The stretch is carved out of the steep hillsides above the ocean, and is equal or superior to the Amalfi and Corniche Drives in Italy, which are world-renowned.

"The most unforgettable natural scene in California is Yosemite Valley, including the side trip through Big Trees, while the man-made site most unique is the hilltop at San Simeon."

*Warren Simmons, chairman of Pier 39's Board of Directors:* "One of my favorite weekend jaunts used to be to go to the Stanislaus River with my wife and children and take an overnight trip down the river on one of the rafts. As my sons got older and could handle a kayak, I obtained kayaks we could ride down the river. I'll never forget those days."

*Melvin Belli, attorney, Law Offices Belli & Choulos:* "My favorite Northern California excursions are Pebble Beach Lodge, Reno and Tahoe, and Yosemite Valley."

*John McEnroe, professional tennis player:* "Northern California is breathtaking. I only wish that during my one year at Stanford I could have had more time to spend off the tennis courts and traveling to the wine country and small towns."

*John Hambrick, former KRON-TV anchorman:* "My favorite retreat of all is a 3-day rafting trip on the American River with my family. Conquering the river with them and strangers, [and] camping out in the evenings, is a unique thrill. I also like the Tahoe area for rest and relaxation."

*Valerie Coleman, present KRON-TV anchorwoman:* "I just like to get into the country. Calistoga is close by with warm summer weather, and it's a great place to unwind."

*Linda "Wonder Woman" Carter:* I'll never forget one of my first trips to Northern California. We hiked up the Marin headlands on the north side of the Golden Gate Bridge. I felt as though I was on top of the world as I looked at the bridge, Alcatraz, Angel Island, the San Francisco Bay, and the city skyline. We picnicked on bread, wine, and cheese."

# 25—RECOMMENDED WEEKEND ADVENTURES

The listings in the preceding chapters have been grouped together according to some basic similarity of interest. This last chapter of the book, however, gathers together the various sights and activities according to geographical location. Places and events close to one another are grouped together in suggested jaunts. Use the geographical index for a complete itemized listing by location.

Some of these trips will take a full weekend or even the increasingly popular 3-day weekend; others fill a day or a half-day. You can expand or tailor these suggested trip outlines to suit your own time and interests.

Remember to make use of maps. Trace out your route before starting any trip. When in doubt about how to get there, ask for directions. Make allowances for weather; it's best not to travel following severe storms, for example, because of flooding, detours, and road blocks. With intelligent planning, you can have a year's worth of weekend adventures.

## TP–1    The City Adventure

San Francisco has 52 weekend activities to enjoy every year. Residents and tourists never tire of what the city has to offer. Jack Shelton's *How to Spend 1 to 10 Perfect Days in San Francisco* (Shelton Publications) is a handy reference book.

If the line is open, be sure to ride the No. 60 Powell-Hyde cable car for spectacular views from some of the steepest hills in the city (see 1-E). At the end of the line you'll be in the Ghirardelli Square area. The National Maritime Museum and old sailing vessels (see 7-A) are nearby. You can take a Bay Cruise or visit the Alcatraz Island (see 3-H and 15-B), or enjoy an Irish coffee at the Buena Vista Cafe.

If you take the No. 59 Powell-Mason cable car line up to Chinatown (see 21-D), be sure to wander off Grant Street onto some of the side streets to get off the beaten track.

The old Italian neighborhood of North Beach is also nearby. Stop in at the Cafe Trieste or Cafe Roma for an espresso and pleasant conversation.

When the weather is good, ride a Muni bus out to Golden Gate Park. The choice of things to do here is endless. You can visit the Japanese Tea Gardens (see

21-F), rent a rowboat to cruise on Stow Lake (see 12-A), explore the M. H. de Young Museum, planetarium, and aquarium, rent horses, or visit the Botanical Gardens for starters.

The western side of Golden Gate Park borders the ocean. A half-mile north of here is the Cliff House, an ideal place to watch the sunset, surfers, and seals while you have a drink (see 3-F).

If you have a car, take the 49-mile scenic drive, making sure to explore the different neighborhoods along the way: Noe Valley, the Richmond, North Beach. Each has a flavor and character all its own.

These are just a few of the pleasures San Francisco offers. Check the geographical index for more suggestions.

## TP-2    From Mudflats to the Mountains (East Bay Area)

This trip will take you 100 miles or more and allow you to enjoy a full day of sights and activities.

Drive east on Highway 80. As soon as you cross the Bay Bridge, you'll see the East Bay Mudflats on your left. For a closer examination of this interesting sculpture, and perhaps an opportunity to meet the artists,

take the Powell Street exit in Emeryville. Follow the road under the freeway and be prepared for possible heavy traffic. Near Scoma's Restaurant, you'll find 400 feet of paved sidewalk parallel to Highway 80. Follow this somewhat muddy road to its end, and you'll find yourself next to animals, castles, missiles, and wooden people.

Back on Highway 80 heading east. Follow signs to Berkeley, then take the University Avenue exit heading east up to the hills. Turn left at Oxford, then right onto Hearst, and right again on Gayley Road. Continue following Rimway and finally Centennial, passing the University Botanical Gardens en route to the Lawrence Hall of Science (see 4-F, 7-I).

On your way back to the freeway, stop for a drive or walk through the campus and along Telegraph Avenue.

Take Ashby Avenue (from Shattuck Avenue) to Highway 24. Drive east and pick up Interstate 680. At Danville, follow signs to Mount Diablo for spectacular sweeping views of up to 35 Northern California counties (see 4-D).

Follow the view with a trip into the sand and silica mine shaft at the Black Diamond Mines Regional Preserve (see 13-E). Quite a contrast! Back on Interstate 680 toward Martinez. Take Route 4 to Alhambra Avenue. (Route 4, heading in the opposite direction, leads to fruit- and vegetable-picking farms in Brentwood. See 8-B.) Turn left under the Alhambra overpass to reach the John Muir Historic Site (see 11-F).

After leaving Muir's, you can spend an hour or several poking around the tiny towns in the hills along the Carquinez Strait. Port Costa, now almost abandoned, was once one of the world's largest wheat-shipping ports. Benicia, on the other side of the strait, makes for fun exploring. This town was the first state capital of California (Benicia was the name of General Vallejo's wife). Start your walking tour near the old Southern Pacific Railroad station. The old Capitol building has now been restored as a state historic park.

The East Bay Hills are filled with miles of trails and open space for hiking, bicycling, and horseback riding. If you want to take advantage of these, contact the East Bay Regional Park District, 11500 Skyline Blvd., Oakland, California 94619.

On the way back to the city, take the Treasure Island turnoff as you cross the Bay Bridge. The sight of San Francisco framed between its two Bay Bridges makes a fitting end to your day.

This trip takes a full day or more. Round trip approximately 100 miles.

## TP–3    Beaches, Birds, and Woods (Marin Coastal Area)

Take U.S. 101 over the Golden Gate Bridge. Instead of the main Sausalito exit, take the Alexander turnoff heading toward this seacoast village. You'll get a good glimpse of Angel Island, Raccoon Straits, and the houses hidden in the hills above you. When the road descends it becomes Bridgeway, Sausalito's main street. You can picnic on the rocks by the water, shop in the boutiques, have a drink on the outside terrace at The Trident, or get an all-encompassing view from the Alta Mira Hotel on Harrison Street (see 4-D).

Back on U.S. 101 heading north. Take the Muir Woods exit, then stroll through this area of gigantic coastal redwoods (see 15-C).

Continue on to Mount Tamalpais. This 2,571-foot mountain offers dozens of trails of varying difficulty and distance. For a relatively small mountain, the views are superior.

Then wind back down and follow signs to California 1 and Stinson Beach (see 3-C). Continue on Route 1 along the Bolinas Lagoon Shore to the Audobon Canyon Ranch to see the great Blue Herons and stunning white egrets (see 5-A).

Take the Olema-Bolinas Road into the town of Bolinas. There, at Duxberry Reef, you can go clamming or tidepooling.

Back to California 1. You'll pass through Olema, once a major sporting center. Now a rural village, Olema is the turnoff for Point Reyes National Seashore headquarters (see 15-F). You can spend hours or even days here.

Leaving Point Reyes take Sir Francis Drake Road, a scenic route in spring, when the landscape is sprinkled with wildflowers. Stop at the Johnson Oyster Company for what residents and tourists call the best oysters in the state. You'll pass the Ten-Mile Beach on your way to Drakes Beach, where you'll probably want to spend the rest of your day.

Return to San Francisco on Sir Francis Drake Boulevard and U.S. 101. Round trip approximately 110 miles.

## TP—4    Small Towns Along the River (Russian River Area)

This trip is an enjoyable two- or three-day adventure less than a tankful of gas from home.

Take U.S. 101 north over the Golden Gate Bridge, past Santa Rosa. Exit on River Road, then drive along the Russian River past several small towns including Rio Nido. Detour to the Armstrong Redwoods State Park and Austin Creek (follow signs) for hiking and picnics.

Continue on River Road to Guerneville, the main town in the Russian River area. Filled with tourists all summer long and teeming with local action in the bars and saloons throughout the year, Guerneville is a great place to while away a few hours. If it's warm enough for a swim, head under the bridge in town to Johnson's Beach (see 1-D). Or rent a canoe for a ride on the little rapids (see 1-G).

Back on River Road for some homemade meals and small-town adventure in Monte Rio. Then you'll pass through Duncan Mills, where you can take a quick side trip to visit the North Pacific Coast Railroad's only remaining depot. Then, in Jenner, relax and take in the view at the River's End Restaurant. Afterwards, head north on California 1 for 13 miles to reach the 19th-century Russian fur trader outpost (see 16-C).

Turn around and drive south on California 1 to the town of Bodega. The place is somewhat eerie; it will probably remind you of Alfred Hitchcock's thriller,

*The Birds,* which was filmed here at Bodega Bay.
   Round trip approximately 160 miles.

## TP–5    Vineyards and Valley of the Moon (Napa and Sonoma)

For the scenic route to the wine country, drive north on U.S. 101 past Santa Rosa to Highway 37 east. Then turn left onto Highway 121 to reach Sonoma. For a taste of this town's colorful past, visit the Sonoma Plaza and General Vallejo's home (see 16-D).

   Take Napa Street east and turn left onto the old Winery Road to get to the Buena Vista Winery (see 9-C). Then head up into the hills on Highway 12 to get to the Jack London State Park in Glen Ellen, where you can visit the House of Happy Walls and the Wolf House. A three-quarter-mile walk takes you to the site of the famous author's grave.

   Back to Highway 121 from Sonoma to Napa. Pick up Highway 29 toward Saint Helena, where you can choose a winery or several for touring and tasting (see chapter 9). There's a deli on the main street in town if you want to pick up a sandwich, then picnic at the nearby community park.

   Continue on Highway 29 past Saint Helena to Dunaweal Lane, then follow signs to Sterling Vineyards. Even if you've had enough wine, you'll want to take the tram up to this winery for a panoramic view of the valley below (see 9-A).

   From Sterling, get back on Highway 29 toward Calistoga for mud baths and hot springs (see 22-C). You can detour to the Petrified Forest along the way. Or follow Highway 128 for about 17 miles to reach California's answer to Yellowstone, the Old Faithful geyser (see 14-D).

   This trip can be a one-, two-, or three-day adventure, depending on how much time you have. Approximately 170 miles round trip.

## TP–6    The Coastal Adventure (Carmel to Big Sur)

This two- or three-day getaway definitely qualifies as a great escape. Don't plan to see museums or use recreational facilities here. Big Sur boasts no commercial tourist attractions, and residents are afraid that too many visitors may ruin the beauty of this dramatic section of California coastline.

   Take California 1 south to Point Lobos, just below Carmel, for a glimpse of the kind of scenery still to come (see 22-B). Then continue on Highway 1. Only the driver should keep his eyes on the winding mountain road. Homes and mansions, rocky cliffs, mountains, and the sea stretch on endlessly from here through Big Sur.

Explore the caves, arches, and waterfalls at Granite Canyon Bridge. Two miles further south is Vista Point, where the tides may be high enough for you to see a blowhole. You'll also drive over the Bixby Creek Bridge, one of the world's highest single-span concrete arch bridges.

As the coastal route begins to pass sand dunes, you'll be able to see the Big Sur Lighthouse. All along the way there are numerous stopping points, and camera buffs especially should take advantage of them.

Nepenthe should not be missed. This is the place to stop and savor all you've seen on your drive as you continue to enjoy this ethereal vision of mountains and sea (see 4-E).

Round trip approximately 300 miles.

## TP-7    Natural Arches, Artichokes, Tame Deer, and Redwoods (Santa Cruz Area)

This can be a weekend jaunt or a pleasant detour on a trip further south.

Pick up California 1 heading south and stop at the Ano Nuevo State Park Reserve for a look at huge coastal mammals (see 17-B).

Then get back on California 1 to Natural Bridges State Park. There are two bridges carved out of the rock by the waves, gracefully curving arches about 35 feet high. You may see painters at work here (see 22-E).

Again back on California 1 to Santa Cruz, left on Chestnut Street following the "Beach" signs, then right on Cliff Drive. You can pause at the grassy park of Lighthouse Point for a wonderful view of the Monterey Bay. Seals bark from an offshore rock.

Again back on California 1, take scenic California 9 north through a thick forest where you'll see the red of the madrone trees. You'll pass through the small but pretty Henry Cowell Redwoods State Park, then the small towns of Felton, Ben Lomond, and the Coulder Creek. Off to the left on California 236 is the larger Big Basin Redwoods State Park.

Big Basin, 12,000 acres of forest, meadows, and canyons, was established in 1902 as the first state park in California (see 15-B). At the park headquarters you may be greeted by deer wandering in from the meadows in hopes of a food handout.

Back on California 1, take the Aptos turnoff for a short detour through the thick walls of redwoods to the Hotel Bay View. Originally built closer to the ocean in 1870 of native redwood, this old hotel was moved here and modernized only to the extent of modern plumbing and lighting. Otherwise, furnishings are the same as when Lillian Russell and King Kalakaua slept here. The hundred-year-old dining room is a favorite attraction of the hotel today.

For a change of pace and scenery, take California 1 to 156 east. You'll arrive in Castroville, a farming town of well-kept homes and ancient buildings. This is the "Artichoke Capital of the World," and you can buy the vegetable fresh from the big artichoke fields.

Head back to San Francisco on Highway 156 and U.S. 101 with a stop at the Stanford University campus in Palo Alto.

Round trip approximately 210 miles.

## TP—8    Father Serra's Grave, Old Monterey, A Scenic Drive (Carmel and Monterey Area)

Take California 1 to Carmel. Turn left on Rio Road-Junipero Avenue for a visit to the Carmel Mission and Father Serra's grave. Be sure to visit the gardens behind the mission. You'll see huge dahlias, fuchsias, and other bright flowers. Then go on into Carmel, the artists' colony. Although the downtown section is usually crowded with tourists, the residential streets are without sidewalks and still have a shaggy look. Stop in at The Tuck Box English Tea Room for breakfast, lunch, or afternoon tea. The scones and homemade preserves are a rare treat.

Then walk down to the beach for a run along the sand or perhaps even a swim.

Then turn left on Ocean Avenue and north on San Antonio Avenue-Carmel Way to the toll gate of the famous 17-Mile Drive (see 19-D).

The drive ends in Monterey for a tour of the old town State Historic Park (see 16-F).

This can be a weekend trip or merely the beginning of a longer vacation down the coast to Southern California with future stops at Big Sur, the Hearst Castle, and Morro Rock.

Round trip approximately 255 miles.

## TP—9    Domes, Waterfalls, Rivers, and Cliffs (Yosemite National Park)

Plan to take at least three days for your trip to Yosemite. If you have time for only one trip a year, this should be it.

Take Highway 80 to 580 to 205 to 120, with a stop for the kids at the Hershey Chocolate Factory and Confectionary Plant (see 18-A).

Pick up the Yosemite Guide upon entering the park, then stop in at the Yosemite Village Visitor Center for a full supply of brochures and maps. With more than 700 miles of trails, you'll need to decipher the maps to figure out what ground you want to cover (see 14-A).

You can rent bicycles for a trip through the valley, walk through a grove of giant Sequoias, the Big Trees, and visit the luxurious Awahnee Hotel.

The Pioneer Center has excellent demonstrations of pioneer crafts. The Yosemite Indian Garden is sprinkled with wildflowers, and during the summer months the Miwok Indians demonstrate old techniques of basket-weaving and grinding acorns.

Ansel Adams spends much of the year at Yosemite with his camera and classes.

If at all possible, avoid Yosemite during June, July, and August. Approximately 185 miles; 370 miles round trip.

## TP—10    Daffodils, Gold, and Grinding Rocks (Gold Country)

You can make this trip at any time of the year, although in winter you'll need chains for the snowy elevations above 2000 feet. Summers are hot and dry, with temperatures ranging from high 80s to high 90s. April is a good month to see the daffodils bloom on Daffodil Hill, just outside of Volcano.

Drive east on Interstate 80 until you get to California 49 (Auburn). Drive south on 49 along the American River. Suggested stops include Coloma (Gold Discovery Site State Park), Amador City, Sutter Creek, and Jackson.

At Jackson, detour east onto California 88 until you get to Pine Grove. Make a left on the Pine Grove-Volcano Road and drive approximately 3 miles to Volcano. Stop first at the Indian Grinding Rocks State Historic Park, about 2 miles before you reach Volcano.

Drive back to Pine Grove and west on 88 to 49. Continue driving south until you get to the Mokelumne Hill ''Historic Loop.''

You can return to the Bay Area from Mokelumne Hill via California 26 to Stockton, then on Interstates 5, 205, and 580.

Allow two to three days. Round trip approximately 296 miles.

Camping available at Folsom Lake and at Indian Grinding Rocks State Historic Park (exception to Grinding Rocks: every fourth weekend in September, during the American Indian Day celebrations).

Breakfast at the Jug and Rose in Volcano.

## TP–11     Sleepy Roads and Moaning Caves (Gold Country)

This trip is best in the fall and spring, but winter trips can be fun if you like to cross-country ski and hike in snowshoes. Be sure to bring along chains for the snowy elevations above 2000 feet. Summers are quite hot and dry, with temperatures reaching into the high 90s and

low 100s. Watch for the Angels Camp annual frog-jumping contest in May (see Chapter 23).

Take Interstates 80, 580, 205, and 5 to Stockton. Take California 4 all the way to the Calaveras Big Trees State Historic Park, with stops in Angels Camp, Murphys, and Mercer Caverns.

If you have time, detour at the Sheep Ranch Road just east of Murphys and make a loop to California 49 at San Andreas.

From San Andreas or Murphys, drive to Sonora. Recommended stops include Moaning Cavern and Columbia State Historic Park.

At Sonora, take the train ride to Jamestown. You can return to the Bay Area via California 120 to Manteca, then Interstates 5, 205, 580, and 80.

Allow two or three days. Approximately 245 miles.

Camping at Calaveras Big Trees State Historic Park.

Breakfast at the Egg Cellar, Parrots Ferry Road, Columbia.

## TP–12     Hidden Beaches, Logging Towns, and Rafting (Lake Tahoe Area)

A weekend in Tahoe is not nearly enough time to spend on the lake or in the heavily-timbered Sierra Nevada. It merely whets your appetite for more. You may want to make two separate trips to the north and south shores.

Drive east on Highway 80 to Highway 267. Stop in Truckee for a walk and perhaps a meal on Commercial Row (the barbecued beef ribs at O'B's Board and the delicious crepes at Grey's Toll Station are too good to pass up). La Vieille Maison, next to the railroad tracks, is a must for lovers of garlic and French cuisine. Truckee has a special Old West flavor, and you can enjoy one or several hours here.

Back on Highway 267 until you reach the lake near King's Beach. If it is late in the day and you arrive before the sun goes down, hurry over to one of the hidden beaches just across the state line (see 12-B). Otherwise you can choose any direction for your 71-mile shoreline trip. You'll get sweeping views and the chance to stop for hikes in the wilderness, jaunts to small coves, or trips on the water (see 12-B).

From Highway 89, heading south, you'll arrive in Tahoe City, an old logging town. Rent a raft from the Truckee River Raft Rentals for a delightful 2 to 2½ hours floating on the Truckee. Then enjoy a cold drink or lunch at the River Ranch, which overlooks Fanny Bridge and the river.

Then detour on Squaw Valley Road to the Tahoe ski area. In summer, you can hike to five different lakes from here (see 12-E).

Back on Highway 89, you'll pass several state parks: Sugar Pine Point, D.L. Bliss, and Emerald Bay (see 21-B).

Desolation Wilderness is a few miles south of Emerald Bay on Highway 89. This area is a haven for experienced hikers.

Back on Highway 89, continue on to the congested commercial South Lake Tahoe area, where activities, restaurants, and casinos are open around the clock. If you enjoy gaming and spend any time in Harrah's, be sure to go up to The Summit Restaurant for a dramatic view of the south shore landscape.

Get home from the south shore via Highway 50 to Highway 80.

Approximately 360 miles round trip.

## TP–13  Country Inns, New England Coast, and the Skunk (Northern California Coastal Area)

This is an ideal trip to make when you want not only to get away, but real peace of mind far away from the problems and pressures of life in the city.

Take U.S. 101 north to Highway 128 just past Cloverdale to California 1. On the way to Mendocino you can stop for some fresh air and stretch your legs at the Salt Point State Park just off California 1.

Get back on California 1 to Little River, an area filled with inns and country lodges. Detour to the Heritage House for a stroll on the grounds out to the ocean overlooks (see 22-A). Then continue on California 1 to Airport Road to visit an old cemetery and the Pygmy Forest (see 14-C). Go on to Mendocino, an arts community with the look of a New England coastal area entirely different from Big Sur (see 10-D).

Continuing north on Route 1, you can "catch-a-canoe" at the Comptiche-Ukiah Road turnoff. Don't ride the canoes in the late afternoon, or the high tides are likely to drain all your strength for the return trip.

Two miles south of Fort Bragg, plant lovers will insist on stopping at the Mendocino Coast Botanical Gardens. There are 47 acres of fuchsias, azaleas, begonias, rhododendrons, and other flowering plants.

Fort Bragg itself is your next stop. This bustling lumber town is nothing like nearby Mendocino; it is the largest coastal city between Eureka and San Francisco. You can go to the railroad station for a ride along the Noyo River on the Skunk (see 20-C), visit the Georgia Pacific Company on Redwood Avenue, or just poke around the old shops.

North on California 1 from there takes you to the end of civilization.

On the trip home, don't leave the coastal route to return to Highway 128. Instead continue on California 1 to visit the Sea Ranch (see 22-D), where modern redwood homes have been built on the rugged coastal bluffs.

Round trip is approximately 340 miles.

## TP–14    Volcanic Parks, Majestic Mountains, and Caves (Far North Area)

This is a two- or three-day adventure for nature lovers.

Take Highway 80 to Interstate 5. At Redding, turn east on Highway 44 toward the Lassen Volcanic National Park. Lassen erupted last in 1915, and during a visit here you're sure to see signs of past volcanic activity. Pick up a brochure at the park's entrance for a list of the various self-guided tours.

Continue on Interstate 5 up to the turnoff for Shasta Caverns, where you can take a boat to begin exploring (see 2-C).

Then back on Interstate 5 to the turnoff for Castle Crags State Park. Summer months are best for climbing on the domes and spires here. Swimming and fishing along the river make excellent afternoon activities.

Back on Interstate 5 for the highlight of this trip north: Mount Shasta (see 14-F). This mountain seems to exert a mysterious power on most visitors and even longtime residents. Be sure to stop in McCloud, an old lumber town at the foot of Mount Shasta, and visit the Mount Shasta Fish Hatchery (see 17-C).

Lake Siskiyou and Castle Lake are good side trips during the summer months. The road to Castle Lake winds through green forests up to a deep blue 47-acre body of water. At both lakes, there's plenty of good fishing, swimming, and camping.

Return home again on Interstate 5 and Highway 80. Round trip approximately 570 miles.

# INDEX BY AREA

# SUBJECT
# INDEX

# SUBJECT INDEX